THE ROWERS' CODE

THE ROWERS' CODE

A Business Parable

How to Pull Together
as a Team—and Win!

By Marilyn Krichko With Jane Rollinson

CAREER
PRESS

Pompton Plains, NJ

THE ROWERS' CODE
Cover design by Lucia Rossman/Digi Dog Design
Printed in the U.S.A.
All photos by Joel W. Rodgers. Illustration on page 118 by Michael Wood.

To order this title, please call toll-free 1-800-CAREER-1 (NJ and Canada: 201-848-0310) to order using VISA or MasterCard, or for further information on books from Career Press.

The Career Press, Inc.
220 West Parkway, Unit 12
Pompton Plains, NJ 07444
www.careerpress.com

Library of Congress Cataloging-in-Publication Data
Krichko, Marilyn.
    The rower's code : a business parable how to pull together as a team-and win! / by Marilyn Krichko ; with Jane Rollinson.
       p. cm.
    Includes bibliographical references and index.
    ISBN 978-1-60163-165-7 -- ISBN 978-1-60163-661-4 (ebook)
      1. Teams in the workplace. 2. Interpersonal communication.
    3. Business communication. I. Rollinson, Jane. II. Title.

HD66.K75 2011
658.4'022--dc22

                                       2010054597

To my sister Jane, who always stands by my side, encourages me, and helps make my life better than I could ever imagine. I could not have a better friend in this world.

Acknowledgments

I would like to thank my friend Laura Peck for getting me to try rowing several years ago in Philadelphia. This whole thing started because of you. It's amazing what one person can do in another person's life. Thank you for all the gut-wrenching rowing experiences I have experienced through the years. I have loved them all— even the ones spent on my rowing machine.

Thank you, Michael Roney, our agent, from Highpoint Executive Publishing (*www.highpointpubs.com*), who not only helped us position our book and find the right publisher, but also provided numerous content architecture and development services.

Thank you, Jon Gordon, for your endless encouragement, inspiration, and support. You are the "Energy Man"!

Thanks to Brenda Snyder and Marti Hamlen for sticking with me all these years—editing material, designing workshops, facilitating in places we never thought we would go—and for your endless friendship through thick and thin. Marti, your editing skills went above and beyond what I ever expected; you are such a gem.

A big thanks to our customers and partners who keep us engaged and who encouraged me to write this book in the first place. Without your continued support and input, this book would never have happened.

Thank you Joel Rogers for your photos throughout the book and Michael Wood for your boat drawing. As they say, a picture is worth a thousand words.

Thank you, Lake Washington Rowing Club, for all your years of encouragement, support, excellent coaching, help with rowing terminology in the book and our workshops' handbooks, and for many happy rowing days. We could not have a better home club at which to facilitate our programs, nor better members and leadership to work with to deliver them successfully. It has taken the effort of several club members working together to make this dream happen. I would especially like to thank Frank Cunningham, Bill and John Tytus, Karyn and Matt Crouthamel, Theresa Batty, Anna Nordstrom, Don Kuehn, Marie Hagman, Elizabeth Burke, Jen Rucier, Lynne Robbins, Rachel Alexander, Marcie Sillman, and the Board of Directors.

Thanks to all the rowing clubs we partner with around the world. It is always an enjoyable experience to meet new coaches and rowers, and we appreciate everything you do to make us feel at home as we deliver our programs when we are not in Seattle.

And finally, a big thanks to Career Press for having the vision to know we were a good fit, listening to our strong opinions, and for believing in this project and making it happen.

Contents

Foreword

Building a Great Team

When I think of building a great team, one word comes to mind: relationships. They are the rock that creates the foundation upon which winning teams are built. After all, the quality of your business and life is determined by the quality of your relationships.

Relationships at work enhance engagement and generate commitment, which in turn fosters great teamwork. If you are thinking that this sounds like common sense, it is. But unfortunately, far too many organizations expect their people to be their best without investing the time and energy to *help* them be their best, nor do they create the relationships that drive success. They want great results but they are not willing to do what it takes to create the relationships and teamwork that deliver them.

And that's where this book comes in. *The Rowers' Code*, and the phenomenally successful workshops on which it is based, is about discovering ways to build a winning team that works together and succeeds together.

Rowing to Greatness

Teams can be one of the most difficult and challenging environments in which to work, which is why they can be so powerful when they work correctly. *The Rowers' Code* suggests a new set of behaviors to help every team and workgroup overcome its greatest challenges and achieve critical goals, offering a powerful blueprint to build the right culture to ensure unprecedented and critical team efficiency.

The workshop does this by putting team members in 60-foot Olympic rowing shells, and, with some expert guidance, these fortunate folks uncover the hidden dynamics of their team and some truths about themselves. Rowing is a powerful metaphor for organizational teamwork, and I can tell you that this experience has been an absolute revelation to the thousands who have spent some time in these boats under the expert guidance of Marilyn Krichko and Jane Rollinson.

The beauty in this is that the rowing metaphor is easy to understand: everyone can picture a boat where the team is rowing together, and everyone can picture a boat where they are not. Rowers' Code participants personalize the analogy, applying it to their own team and individual roles. It's brilliant!

Marilyn identified this game-changing concept while taking a rowing class at the University of Pennsylvania back in the 1990s, just prior to her assuming a key corporate position in Europe. Eventually the revelation changed her life, and in 1998 she created the Rowers Code and founded the OARS program to deliver teambuilding workshops using rowing around the globe.

Since then, the Rowers' Code has had a profound, immediate impact on thousands of people, teams and their leaders, with scores of Fortune 500 clients lining up to participate in the workshops and reap the benefits of team success.

The book you hold in your hands mirrors the workshops themselves, giving anyone who reads it a deep, useful, and highly satisfying taste of the experience. Like the workshops and speaking engagements, it provides a framework to consider where your personal strengths and weaknesses lie, and how you can improve your own team performance.

Get in the Boat

Being a highly capable individual—one with talent, knowledge, skills, and good work habits—is not enough these days. Individuals in your organization must also be contributing team members, augmenting the achievement of group objectives and working effectively with others in a collaborative setting.

It all comes down to this: every team needs a code; not a simple list of values, but *a practical guide for unlocking each person's potential to unleash the effectiveness of the group*! Well, here it is.

During the past several years I have written extensively, most notably in my best-selling books *The Energy Bus* and *Soup*, about ways to build strong, effective teams and that all-important culture of greatness. The Rowers' Code is part of the progression—the logical next step in any team's development.

You can take it from me: you've driven the bus; now get in the boat. It's time to start rowing!

—Jon Gordon

Wall Street Journal best-selling author of
The Energy Bus and *Soup*

February 2011

Preface

One summer in Philadelphia, a young woman was asked by a friend to take a rowing class at the University of Pennsylvania. She didn't have much free time, so she declined, thinking she couldn't make the commitment. She had just been promoted to an executive position and had much to do in order to get ready to move to Germany, including several hours of German business language tutoring every day. Her friend persisted, and she finally gave in and agreed to take the rowing class. After the first few minutes she was in the boat with eight other people, she began to understand the power of the metaphor of rowing, and eventually it changed her life.

I am that young woman, only now it is several years later, and I have a story to tell that I hope inspires you.

—Marilyn Krichko

19

"If you could get all the people in an organization rowing in the same direction, you could dominate any industry, in any market, against any competition, at any time."

—From *The Five Dysfunctions of a Team*
by Patrick Lencioni

Prologue

Sea of Change

Recently, in a city in the great Northwest, eight people who worked together on a team were faced with challenges like never before. The economy had gone from boom to bust in a short period of time. To meet the demands of the new economy, every company, including their own, not only needed to cut costs and trim the fat, but they also needed a solid plan in place for how to move forward.

Change was happening all around them. Just as their team was starting the process of putting a new plan together, their boss of several years moved to a new division. Spirits were low. As a team, they were not sure how they would pull together and come up with a plan that would work. As individuals, they were afraid of losing their jobs. They needed a plan that would bring them through these hard times. They could only hope their new boss would be able to lead them through the sea of change.

Chapter 1

The Big Idea

As Christine sat in traffic on the Montlake Bridge in Seattle, she was thinking about her new job and the upcoming strategic-planning meeting when her eyes shifted focus to the water below. There she noticed the University of Washington crews out for their morning row. It was a beautiful day; the sun was just rising over the mountains and a light fog was lifting off the lake. The crew teams seemed like graceful swans as they glided by in their sleek rowing shells.

Christine found it fascinating to watch. Her sister rowed at Princeton and Christine reminisced about the excitement surrounding the regattas she had attended a few years ago. Being on the crew team meant so much to her sister, who had developed close relationships with her teammates through the years. They stuck together through good times and bad. Christine thought about how close her sister's team was.

Christine was confident in her strong leadership capabilities, but she was new to the team, so she still had to gain her team's trust, as well as figure out where their strengths were. Then the idea struck her: *What if my new team gets into a boat like that and learns to row together? Maybe it would give us a different way of looking at things and some new ideas to help us move forward successfully.*

The Memo

The next day, Christine told her best friend, Anna, about her big idea. Anna remembered reading an article in *Spectrum* magazine about a company in Seattle, Criterion Consulting Solutions, which used rowing in teambuilding workshops.

Anna forwarded the article to Christine, who was impressed by what she read. By that afternoon, Christine had enrolled her team in a one-day Rowers' Code workshop at Lake Washington Rowing Club in Seattle. She was so excited that she wished the program could start immediately. She hoped her team would feel the same way.

Christine sent a memo out to the team the next day:

Good Morning Team!

Our strategic-planning meeting is only a few weeks away. As is tradition, we will kick off the meeting with a teambuilding activity the first day. The second day we will start working on our new strategic plan. This year's teambuilding activity is Olympic-style rowing.

We should all be familiar with the analogy of rowing together in the same direction, and we will have a chance to try it ourselves in a 60-foot-long rowing shell at the Lake Washington Rowing Club in Freemont.

I'm excited about our time together and am certain that great things will come from our high-quality interactions.

I'll be sending out a another memo with an agenda and other details, but if you have any questions or concerns in the meantime, please contact our facilitator, Angela Smith, at Criterion Consulting Solutions.

Thanks again for being a valued member of the team!

—Christine

Some of the team members were pleased when they opened Christine's e-mail and read what they were going to do for the annual teambuilding activity. Chip in Marketing was especially happy. He loved physical challenges where he could show off, and once again he would get his chance. Having been with company for years, Chip had developed an unlimited confidence in his leadership abilities— sometimes to a fault.

Nancy in Operations was pleased as well, intrigued by the idea of trying a new sport. She enjoyed working in teams, especially on tough projects. This activity presented enough of challenge to pique her interest.

Immediately after Marie, a Senior Project Manager, read the e-mail, she started searching the Internet for more information. She wanted to know everything she could about rowing. She did everything, at work and at play, with intensity, and often expected quick, fabulous results.

Peter in Finance, the newest member of the team, thought it was cool that they were going to do something so different. It would give him a chance to get to know the others—and for them to get to know him. So far he had been reticent in his interactions with the others, preferring to study them from afar at first, but hoped to become an integral part of the team soon.

Dave in Legal and Government Affairs had mixed feelings. He liked teambuilding activities, but wasn't so sure about rowing. In fact, Dave wasn't so sure about many things in his professional life, and often relied on others to take the lead, which sometimes led to success, but other times caused problems.

Tim in IT had a different reaction to the e-mail, laughing out loud when he read it; he just couldn't picture their boat going anywhere if they were all in it together. This was the first time Tim had laughed in a while. Tim was a worrier who took his professional and personal responsibilities seriously. Recently, an incident at work caused him to be even more worried about his job and its future.

Doug, Vice President of Sales, laughed and put the whole thing straight out of his mind. *What a waste of time*, he said to himself as he sat shaking his head. Doug was concerned with his sales, but not much else at his company. He grew up spoiled, and he carried this into his professional life, doing what he pleased at every opportunity with little regard for others.

Summary and Key Concepts

- Being challenged in a new way can give team members a profoundly different view of how they work with others. It spurs new ideas of how to move forward successfully.

- Team members approach challenges in unique ways. Individuals will each bring their own preconceptions, emotions, and goals to a new challenge. Some will be enthusiastic, while others will approach a new challenge with lesser levels of confidence, or insecurity, as well as other personal traits.

Chapter 2

The Offsite

The team allocated two days for their offsite: one day for teambuilding and one day to start working on their new strategic plan. The agenda stated that they would begin each day at 9 a.m. and finish by 5 p.m., so they could have a team dinner in the evening.

On the first day of the offsite, everyone arrived at the rowing club with ample time to begin promptly at 9 a.m. The club was founded in 1957 by athletes training for international competition. With rowing shells in the boat bays on the first floor and unequaled views of downtown Seattle and Mt. Rainier from the second floor balcony, it was an impressive facility. The team had been instructed to wear clothing that was suitable for biking, so their clothes wouldn't get caught in any of the rowing gear. But not everyone came in sports clothes—Doug arrived wearing a suit.

The workshop facilitator, Angela, stood in front of them with a big smile on her face. "Welcome to the Rowers' Code Program," she began. "Today you will learn to row in an Olympic-style rowing boat called an '8.' It gets that name because it holds eight rowers, plus someone who steers. Teamwork is key, because, in an 8, everything you do or don't do affects the other people in the boat.

"I'll introduce you to the seven principles of the Rowers' Code, which you can use to guide your actions and help you stay focused on what's important. This will be a new experience, like none you have ever had before, so I hope you enjoy it and take something back to the office that is life-changing."

To Angela, this group looked like any other group. There was always someone who didn't read the e-mail or come prepared to row. Doug was certainly not dressed for the occasion.

Doing What's Best

"We will start by learning few things about your boat," she said. "It's 60 feet long and weighs 235 pounds." Angela explained that it was very important for the team to work together, even when taking the boat in and out of the boathouse and putting it in and out of the water, so no one would get hurt. "If everyone carries their load, each person will only be carrying about 30 pounds. If you don't do your part, the weight will fall on someone else, and that someone may get hurt."

Doug raised his hand.

"Yes, Doug," Angela said as she assessed his suit.

"We've been having some serious budget problems and I was planning on working on them while everyone else went out in the boat," he declared, as he sat up in his chair. "So, I didn't bring any clothes to row in. I hope that won't be a problem." Eyebrows raised around the room as everyone looked to Angela for a response.

With a thoughtful look on her face, Angela quickly replied, "I think this is a good time to introduce the first point in the Rowers' Code."

She wrote on the white board:

#1 Always Do What's Best for the Team.

"Doug, I know you have some work you think you need to do right now, but your team needs you to fill a seat in the boat. It's really not going to work if you don't all get in together."

Their new boss, Christine, spoke up. "Yes, I agree. We really need everyone to actively participate. That means putting aside your own agendas and sticking to the one we all agreed to. Is that going to be a problem for anyone else?"

No one said a word. They all just stared at Doug, waiting for his response. The air was thick and Doug felt the pressure. "Okay," he said, "I'm in."

Perfect, thought Nancy. *He's always so passive-aggressive. I can't believe he thought he could show up today wearing his suit and get out of this.*

She remembered the teambuilding event the year before when Doug had said he couldn't hike up Mt. Rainier because he forgot his hiking shoes. That time they all went for a day hike, while he caught up on e-mail in the lodge. *He just doesn't get it,* she thought. Then she recalled a college lecture from the renowned physicist Richard Feynman, during which he said, "This is about things you know nothing about." Looking around the room at her teammates, she knew that getting in one boat together and working as a team would definitely be about things they knew nothing about.

Angela showed the team a rowing video and explained the basic rowing stroke. In the video, the rowers were perfectly synchronized. They made the activity look easy, maybe even fun. The rowers had determined looks on their faces. The crew moved as one, with each person doing his or her part to keep it together.

A few times Angela paused the video to show the workshop participants each part of the stroke: the catch, the drive, and the finish. The motions were perfectly aligned. It was beautiful. Everyone was anxious to give it a try, even though they knew they would not look like the expert rowers in the video their first time out.

Summary and Key Concepts

Rowers' Code:	Meaning:	Core Principle:
#1 Always Do What's Best for the Team.	Putting the interests of your team in front of your own. Rowing as "one boat" instead of everyone rowing in his or her own direction.	Commitment

- ♦ The Rowers' Code is a simple, actionable set of behaviors about teamwork and communication that can be applied to every workplace scenario. It is based on the premise that everything you do or don't do affects others. The Rowers' Code will guide your actions and help keep you focused on what's important.

- ♦ Having a sense of common purpose is what brings teams together in the first place. Staying focused and putting the team first can be a huge challenge. No one individual brings everything to the table to ensure success, so it takes every team member putting the team first to build a successful team.

Chapter 3

The Line-Up

Angela continued her presentation. "As I mentioned, there are nine seats in the boat—eight for rowers and one for someone to steer. Your task during the next 30 minutes is to figure out the right seat for each person so that you maximize the strengths of your team."

She distributed a handout. "Here are the descriptions of the seats in the boat. We will use these with the radar charts in your workbooks to map your strengths and weaknesses so you can capitalize on your strengths and mitigate your weaknesses as a team."

The charts looked like this:

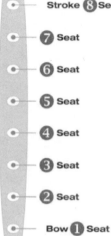

Coxswain: Allocates resources to get equipment and people where they need to be; maps out the course; steers the boat; gives feedback; keeps control; motivates; acts strategically; pushes the team to do their best.

8 (Stroke): Leads; knows how to pace the team; has a high level of skill and strength; effective and efficient; wants to get the job done well.

7: Similar to stroke; works in tandem on the other side of the boat.

6, 5, 4, and 3: The powerhouse consists of the strongest rowers in the boat; able to follow the leader and concentrate on keeping pace while not pushing others to go too fast up the slide; want to get the job done.

2 and 1 (Bow): Affects the balance of the boat the most; must be able to anticipate and keep pace with the others; finds ways to keep the boat balanced.

Seat descriptions for an "8" rowing shell

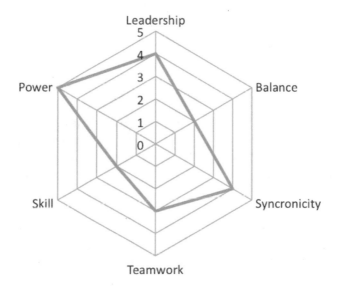

The radar chart

On the Radar

The workbooks explained how to use the radar charts to map their personal strengths and weaknesses. There were six levels to the scale. Marking an item with a 0 meant the item was a weakness, whereas 5 meant it was a strength. It was relatively easy for the team to fill in the radar charts, because each person knew his or her own strengths and weaknesses. However, some people had not developed enough trust to share the truth with the team.

Marie, like many others, drew a chart she thought the team would expect her to. She was afraid to share her true thoughts because doing that wouldn't win her any brownie points with Christine or the rest of the team. Her drawing indicated that she put the team first, but, in reality, she had no intention of putting anyone first but herself. She knew that such an attitude would sound selfish, especially because Doug had just been chastised for trying to put his own interests first, so she lied. *Big deal,* she thought. *Life is tough. You have to fight for yourself.* Putting herself first was the only way she would get to the front of the line.

Marie always remembered her father's advice: "If you want to be number one, you have to look out for yourself, because no one else will." Her father etched it into her brain. "Day in, day out. Be number one, Marie." She could still hear his voice.

She was already 31 years old, so where was the big promotion she had dreamed of? Where was her private jet? Her Maserati? Vacations to the south of France? Shopping trips in London? She desperately wanted to get to the front of the line.

But how? How did her friend Renee do it? Marie had spent countless hours listening to Renee's stories of her executive job in Europe. She traveled to cities Marie could only dream of. Renee had a wonderful life, a dream job, and all the things that went with it, including a driver who picked her up from the Zurich airport for weekends when Renee felt like coming home to her house in the foothills of the Alps. The rest of the time she gallivanted around Europe at the company's expense. It was so romantic, that pleasant executive lifestyle.

Marie wanted in too. She wanted to be part of the privileged elite; she wanted to be the queen of the mountain. She craved it and was determined to get there at any cost. She just didn't know how to do it...yet.

As her thoughts returned to the team, she realized there were a few points she could be honest about without hurting anyone's feelings; she trusted in herself and in her leader, Christine. Marie felt as though she did her share and thought she was good at communicating clearly. Those were clearly things she could be truthful about without anyone getting their knickers in a twist.

Marie plotted a few mid-range answers on her radar chart to even things out. *I'm sure we won't have time to scrutinize our charts anyhow*, she thought. And she was right. The team had moved on to figuring out the right seats to maximize their strengths as a team. They hardly paid attention to their radar diagrams and the valuable information they could provide.

Marie's radar chart

Jockeying for Position

Although the seat descriptions were easy to understand, it was difficult for some of the team members to select their seats. As they started their discussion, it was clear that Chip wanted the "leadership" spot—the 8 seat or "stroke." As always, no one felt like arguing with him. When they had stood up to him in the past, it never paid off. That left the 7 seat as another leadership position, which most of them thought Christine would probably take, although she was quiet during the initial discussion so she could hear what her team had to say. Seats 6, 5, 4, and 3 were the "powerhouse" seats, and several of the team members wanted to get into 6 seat in order to be at the front of the powerhouse. Seats 2 and 1, the bow seats, had "balance" associated with them, not power, so no one wanted those.

While everyone was talking, Christine got a text message and left the room.

After several minutes, Angela asked them to go up to the white board and write their names next to the seats they thought suited them best. Here's what they wrote:

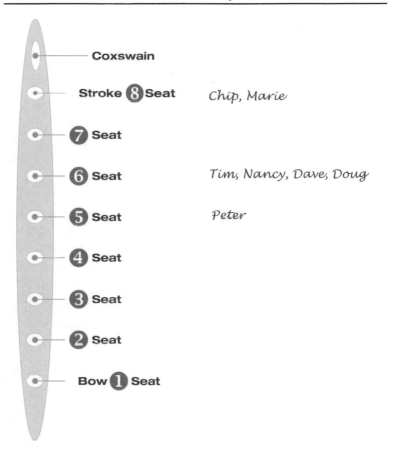

After looking at the results, Chip spoke up. "Wow, it seems like a few of us want the same seats. We can't have two people in the same seat, so let's sort that out first."

In the next few minutes he jockeyed his way into the stroke seat and pushed Marie back to 6 seat by making an argument for Dave in 7 seat.

Marie was upset. She wanted so badly to be in the stroke seat as the leader. To prepare for the offsite she had spent hours doing research on rowing so she would know exactly what an Olympic rowing stroke looked like. Every night for the past three weeks she practiced on the rowing machine at the gym so she could set an example for her team. Now her chance had faded; she would have to settle for 6 seat. Once again, Chip won out. *I should be stroke,* she thought. *They just don't know how great I am.*

After that, no one had much to say. Chip took control and managed to get everyone into the seats for which he felt they were best suited, or the seats that suited his own agenda.

Summary and Key Concepts

♦   Mapping the strengths and weaknesses of team members gives the team a baseline to work from and helps the team make sure they have the right fit for the task at hand.

♦   If there are too many people in one seat, or if there are empty seats, it helps the team realize overlap and gaps so they can be addressed and the team can maintain balance.

Chapter 4

Mistakes Happen

When Christine returned, it was time to explain the line-up to Angela. As she looked up at the white board she couldn't believe her eyes. They had put her in 4 seat. She couldn't understand how she ended up back there instead of upfront in the stroke seat. After all, she was the leader of the team. The leadership seat was the natural place for her to be in!

When she had stepped out of the room to make a phone call, she assumed they would put her up in front as their leader. How embarrassing! It was her idea to row in the first place! She hated the seat they had given her. It made her feel almost betrayed. She realized she shouldn't have dropped the ball at such a critical point in the process.

All kinds of thoughts ran through Christine's head as she tried to figure out how this could have happened.

On one hand, she knew the team members appreciated her. On the other, she wondered if maybe they didn't understand all the time and effort she put into her team. Maybe they didn't understand how complex her job was with all the responsibilities someone in her position was constantly juggling and negotiating on their behalf. Maybe Chip was trying to position himself as the new leader.

She had been hired her for her work ethic, leadership style, and ability to succeed. But, was she succeeding? In her initial meetings with the team, Chip challenged her on several issues. It seemed she and Chip had different ideas about how to move forward. But, he worked for her, and she was the boss.

Right now, she didn't feel like the boss, though. She told herself to calm down and get her head back in the game. It would be fine. Besides it wasn't just about her, it was about her team. *Be a good sport*, she told herself. *You don't always have to lead from the front. You can lead from behind.*

Final Seat Selections

Chip took the lead again and explained why each person was in his or her respective seat. He spoke a lot about leadership in the front of the boat, then stressed the importance of following in the middle and of balance in the back.

He didn't say it, but the way Chip figured it, the last two seats were for patsies. That's where he put Doug and Peter, the new guy. Chip put Dave in 7 seat, even though it wasn't the best seat for him. Dave had back-stabbed him the week before and Chip wanted his colleague to have to sit right behind him to put him in his place.

Nancy, the athlete, should have been in stroke or 7 seat, but Chip didn't want her to make him look bad. He orchestrated her into the last seat in the powerhouse right next to Doug. That would be hard for her because Doug probably wouldn't even try and it would drive her crazy.

But Nancy was okay with her seat. It would give her a chance to see what the people in front of her were doing and encourage them if she thought they were out of sync with the stroke and 7 seat. Peter, being new to the team, did exactly what Chip wanted, taking the last seat without a peep.

At the end of his explanation to Angela, Chip asked if anyone objected. No one spoke up; not even Christine or Marie. Here was the line-up:

Coxswain	
Stroke 8 Seat	Chip
7 Seat	Dave
6 Seat	Marie
5 Seat	Tim
4 Seat	Christine
3 Seat	Nancy
2 Seat	Doug
Bow 1 Seat	Peter

Final seat selections

Angela waited to see how the team would react to Chip's line-up. When no one said a word, she asked, "Is everyone happy with the line-up?"

"Yes," Chip responded confidently, looking around at the team. Again, no one challenged him. Angela had experienced this type of overpowering behavior several times before with other groups. It was clear that Chip valued some seats more than others just by the way he discussed each seat assignment during his explanation of the line-up. She continued, "I think it's time to introduce the second point in the Rowers' Code."

#2 Give Every Seat Equal Value.

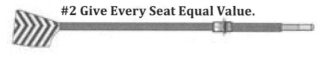

"It's important to value people and tap into their strengths to come up with the best combination, so the boat performs its best," she explained. "Each seat has a role that's specific to that seat. A crew needs every seat in the boat to perform at its best to win the race." Several of the participants looked thoughtful, but no one said a single word.

She asked, "Is this the best combination? Did you tap into everyone's strengths?" Everyone sort of nodded. However, Angela sensed that individuals' strong points were not really considered in their seat selections. It seemed as if they were just trying to hurry up and get out on the water.

Angela wasn't hearing valid arguments for why each person was selected for his or her boat seat. *This is definitely a sign that this team needs help*, Angela thought. *Is this the best combination? Did they use their strengths and mitigate their weaknesses in picking their seats? Probably not. But, it's their boat, and they have to row it.*

In reality, Christine and Marie wanted to be up in the front in stroke or 7 seat. Nancy was hoping Christine and someone other than Chip would step up and lead the team. Dave was okay being in 7 seat. He had wanted to be in the powerhouse instead of being one of the leaders, but he was fairly good at sports and thought it would give him a chance to do something for the team.

Peter didn't want to rock the boat before he got to know everyone, so he kept his mouth shut, but was beginning to realize that Chip was a bit of a bully. Doug put his name by 6 seat so everyone would think he wanted to try hard. He was happy when Chip put him in 2 seat behind Nancy. She was strong and would carry him, making it a bit easier. He still thought the whole thing was stupid and was upset about having to row in his suit, but he couldn't do anything about that now. Tim would have been happy with any seat in the powerhouse, and that's just what he got: a seat right in the middle of it.

It seemed like the line-up was set. They were all waiting to row. Angela was waiting for someone to acknowledge that they didn't have anyone to steer when it was time for them to make their way to the boathouse to meet their coach.

"Ok," Angela said. "I guess this is our line-up. Let's get rowing."

When they got to the boathouse, Nancy spoke up. "Who is going to steer? We are one person short."

Angela smiled. "I thought you'd never ask. I've invited a good friend and fellow rower, Kim, to join us today. She's helping your coach get his boat ready right now. I think you'll like her; she's a four-time Olympic gold medalist and a really good sport."

A few of the team members realized that they had made a big mistake in the way they set their boat. If they had brought up the empty seat sooner, they could have had the advantage of using the Olympic rower in the 8 seat as their example to follow. Now it was too late; it was time to row.

Summary and Key Concepts

Rowers' Code:	Meaning:	Core Principle:
#2 Give Every Seat Equal Value.	Treating others with respect. Acknowledging and trusting in each other's strengths.	Acknowledgment

♦ Being present and engaged is every team member's responsibility during decision-making. Encouraging team participation by supporting behaviors such as active listening, summarizing key points, asking clarifying questions, and soliciting reactions will help you. Also, make sure you eliminate distractions such as talking on cell phones, leaving the room, reading e-mails, and doing other multi-tasking, to keep everyone focused on the task at hand.

♦ Team success relies on valuing people and tapping into their strengths. To tap into the strengths of your team, find out what knowledge, skills, and experience people have in relation to the task at hand. If you have access to a subject-matter expert, take advantage of his or her expertise.

Chapter 5

Hands On

Right before their eyes was a beautiful racing shell, with the name *Pocock Racing* painted in gold letters on the side. They all stood staring at the boat in awe. Chip took a deep breath, turned to Dave, and confidently said, "We can do this."

Dave forced a smile back. He was scared. Although he was tall and looked strong, Dave wasn't really very coordinated at all. *If Chip can do this, I can do this*, he kept telling himself, hoping it would invoke some self-confidence.

Nancy was excited. She had looked forward to this day from the moment she received the memo. This was great; not only did she get to have fun during work, but she also had the bonus of being able to try a new sport!

Angela saw the mixed emotions on the faces in front of her, and thought it was time to get moving and hand the team over to their coach. Just then, their coach walked into the boathouse. They all looked up at him. He stood 6' 4", tall, with light hair. He was strong and looked like he could carry one of the big boats all by himself. Kim accompanied him.

"Hi everyone, my name is Bill Carlson. I'll be your coach for the day. Now, everyone, listen up. There are a few things we need to cover so that you can get your boat out of the boathouse and onto the water without anyone getting hurt. This involves the third point in the Rowers' Code.

#3 Carry Your Load.

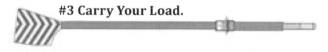

"The boat weighs 235 pounds, and the weight needs to be evenly distributed while it's being carried. You don't want to hurt your teammates by not doing your share," he continued. "So, I'll need your absolute attention while we are taking the boat out of the house and putting it on the water. There are a series of commands that Kim will use to help you work as a team. By looking at your line-up, I see you have put Kim in the coxswain position."

Angela saw the surprised look on Kim's face when Bill announced she was the coxswain. Considering all the talent and experience she had, she couldn't believe they'd picked her to steer the boat instead of helping them row. Although they were not maximizing Kim's strengths and using her as the perfect example of a rower to follow, she could contribute in any seat in the boat and didn't mind steering at all. At least they would have the benefit of someone steering who knew what they were doing.

Critical Commands

Bill spent the next few minutes covering the commands used to get the boat safely into the water:

- **Count off when ready.** Count off by your seat number when you are ready, starting with stroke and ending with bow. This is so the coach and coxswain know that everyone is ready.

- **Hands on.** Put your hands on the boat, and get ready to pick it up.

- **Up and overhead.** Lift the boat up over your head.

- **Split to sides.** Move to the sides of the boat, alternating people on the port and starboard sides.

- **Down to shoulders.** Lower the boat down to your shoulders

- **Walk it out.** Watching the riggers, walk the boat out of the boathouse and down to the water.

- **Up and overhead.** Lift the boat up over your head.

- **Toes to the edge.** Walk to the edge of the dock with the boat up overhead.

- **Grab hold and roll to high waist.** While hanging on to the boat, roll it over and hold it out over the water at waist height.

- **Set it in.** Set the boat in the water.

As Bill was explaining each command, Kim showed the team what they would be doing. This was all new vocabulary for the group, and it made most of them a little nervous about being able to execute on command.

Doug was daydreaming a bit and wasn't really paying attention. When it was time to move the boat, he was gazing absentmindedly at his feet. To engage him, Kim gently put her hand on his back on gave him a little nudge. "Ok, let's go, team. Count off when ready."

They mumbled their seat numbers one by one. "That won't do," Kim shouted, "Come on, put some gusto into it." Chip was hoping everyone would follow, so he shouted out at the top of his lungs "Stroke!" Luckily everyone followed, in order of their seat, "7, 6, 5, 4, 3, 2, bow."

Now they sound like they should, thought Kim.

Sharing the Load

Kim shouted, "Hands on," and they immediately put their hands on the boat. After getting it up and overhead, and putting it on their shoulders, they slowly started walking it out of the boathouse and down to the water. They were not all the same height, which made the boat feel heavier for some than for others.

The previous week, Peter had finished a course of antibiotics for a sinus infection, and he didn't feel quite right yet. He was afraid he wouldn't have enough physical strength for the exercise, and he didn't want to disappoint anyone. Being the new guy, this was important to him. He was also afraid that Chip and some of the guys didn't like him, which might explain how he ended up in the last seat in the boat. He hoped it wasn't a sign of what they thought about him.

He realized that, at that moment, he felt cut off from the team. *That's weird,* he thought, *Here I am carrying a huge boat down to the water with my teammates during a team exercise and I feel alone. This is exactly how I feel at work sometimes.* He decided to focus on the task at hand and not let it bother him.

Carrying the boat was not as easy as they all thought. The team of eight had to focus on working together to keep the boat level in order to get it out of the boathouse, down the ramp, and to the water's edge.

The ramp was narrow. To avoid damage to the boat, it had to be turned slightly on its side until they all had their feet on the dock below. At times Doug and a few others felt as though they were carrying the boat for some of the people around them. Doug wondered if anyone else felt the same way, but he was afraid to say something after his suit fiasco. He didn't want to be labeled a whiner. He was still waiting for a magic moment to occur that would get him out of the exercise so he could go and get some work done.

For the rest of them, everything felt unfamiliar, and they could only focus on what they were told to do at that very moment. They were experiencing both fear of the unknown and the excitement of learning to row in an Olympic-style rowing boat. As they put their toes to the edge of the dock and lowered the boat, a feeling of accomplishment overtook them all.

"We did it!" They yelled, "Way to go! Wahoo!" Several high-fives went around. Everyone was pleased with their success, especially Christine.

Summary and Key Concepts

Rowers' Code:	Meaning:	Core Principle:
#3 Carry Your Load.	Knowing and doing your share of what needs to be done.	Responsibility

♦ With teamwork, even the heaviest load can be negotiated with success. Sometimes, it's the small things that can make a team member feel either part of the team or left out. Understanding what you are expected to do, and acknowledging the contributions of others, helps bring the team closer together and gives everyone a sense of purpose.

Chapter 6

No Turning Back

The boat sat low in the water like a kayak, but at 60 feet long and less than 2 feet wide, it was much more impressive. Doug tried telling himself that rowing this sleek, carbon-fiber craft wouldn't be so difficult. But standing there on the dock, looking at the state-of-the-art 8 he realized that it looked, well...frighteningly narrow and unstable. The experience facing him would be far more challenging than he originally thought—not anything like kayaking or any teambuilding activity he had ever done before. The thought of rowing backwards while sitting on a moving seat in this long skinny shell in tandem with seven other people became terrifying.

One Foot In

After learning how to put their oars in the oarlocks and adjust their foot stretchers, it was time to get into the boat as a team.

Standing next to the group on the dock, Kim instructed them on how to proceed. "There is only one place for each of you to step when you get into the boat," she shouted, straining to make her voice heard above the noise of a passing motorboat. "If you don't step in that exact place, your foot will go through the bottom of the boat. So, pay attention."

They were all shocked when they heard the words "go through the bottom of the boat." Most boats they had been in prior to this experience weren't so fragile. Kim pointed to where they should step as they all paid attention—no one wanted to damage the boat.

As Doug looked out at the lake, it suddenly seemed so busy. Seaplanes were buzzing overhead, boats were motoring by, and his head felt fuzzy. He realized there was no turning back. For a brief moment he imagined what would happen if he just ran away. He wanted to turn and bolt, but his feet wouldn't budge. They stayed firmly planted on the dock.

Marie's experience was vastly different from Doug's. She looked out at the boat and dreamed of what it would feel like if they really got the 8 moving. After all, she didn't buy her rowing outfit for nothing.

Kim continued, "You'll start by grabbing hold of your oar and placing one foot in the boat. Each team member has one—and only one—place to put your foot. When I call it, saying 'one foot in,' you'll grab hold of your oar, put one foot on the spot I showed you, swing your other foot into the foot stretcher, and sit down." It sounded easy, but it was complicated, and they were all worried they would mess it up.

The team lined up next to the boat, and when they were ready, called off their seat numbers. Kim called out the command, "Grab hold of your oar, one foot in, and down. And down."

It was perfect. Just as they were instructed, they grasped their oars with one hand, stepped on the right spot, swung their other foot around, gripped the gunnel with their free hand for support, and sat down.

Chip was impressed with himself and the team. Tim, however, was shaking a bit. He'd almost stepped on the wrong spot, which would have cost them. Bill told them earlier that the boat they were rowing in cost more than $30,000.

Safe in their seats, most of them were afraid to move. The boat seemed much narrower now that they were in it. It all seemed so foreign: the boat, the riggers, the very long oars, having their feet in shoes attached to the boat. The team was filled with anxious excitement. Bill let them sit there for a few minutes to get used to their seats and the feeling of being in the boat together.

"Good job!" Kim proclaimed. "Now, each of you has just one oar to be responsible for. Your seats slide on tracks, which means you have to be very careful not to rap the person in front of you in the back with your oar! We are almost ready to push off from the dock, so I need everyone to focus. Any distraction can easily render the whole experience miserable for everyone. Your team is relying on you."

Balancing the Boat

They sat waiting for instructions as their coach pulled up next to their boat in his launch, a motorized boat he would use to follow them. "It's time to introduce the next part of the Rowers' Code," Bill announced.

#4 Balance the Boat.

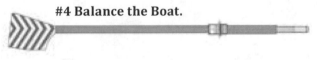

"Your equipment is designed for maximum efficiency," Bill told the team. "If you work with it properly, it will pay off and you'll glide like a swan. If you don't, you will fight a losing battle and tire yourselves out. Don't waste your energy fighting with your own equipment.

"Your oar is the one tool you have to move the boat," he added, driving home the point. "Your efficiency with it will determine how fast you go. Your oars are suspended by the riggers," he continued. "Using your oars correctly can also help you balance the boat. Make small adjustments and focus on doing the right things because even small changes have an exponential affect on the team. And there's one more thing you should remember: never let go of your oar!"

Chip looked down at his oar handle. It seemed so simple when they were on dry land. Now that they were out on the lake in the boat, it didn't seem so simple anymore.

Bill explained further that with their sliding seats they could push with their legs while rowing, using the strongest muscles in their bodies, adding, "It's really important to move in tandem with the person in front of you, maximizing teamwork instead of trying to do your own thing. Don't even think of trying to be a maverick. It won't work."

Everyone concentrated on Bill's instructions, and some of them began to feel a little more comfortable in their seats. But they weren't rowing yet. They weren't even off the dock. They waited, knowing the moment of truth was not far away. Bill explained that they would do a few exercises to help them balance the boat once they pushed off from the dock.

Summary and Key Concepts

Rowers' Code:	Meaning:	Core Principle:
#4 Balance the Boat.	Attaining the right mix of people and skills on your team to meet your goals.	Organizational and self-awareness

♦ Balance is the ability to hold calm and steady, adding stability to your team's overall efforts. It is easier to attain when you have the knowledge of what to do, are careful when it matters, and work in sync with your team-mates. Understanding your resources and how to use them is key to organizational success.

♦ Make small adjustments and focus on doing the right things, because even small changes have an exponential effect on the team.

Chapter 7

Moment of Truth

"Is everyone ready?" Bill asked. They all stared blankly at him. They looked almost frozen in their positions in the boat with all its moving parts. He smiled at their nervousness, knowing what it was like to be this anxious. Every novice crew experiences the uneasy feeling of pushing off from the dock for the first time.

As Bill gave them some final instructions, even Chip and Marie weren't feeling so confident anymore. "Okay then, Kim, have them count off when ready, and then you can shove off from the dock."

No, thought Doug, *Please no. I want to stay on dry land.* But no one heard his plea, of course. No one knew what anyone else was thinking. It was time to get moving.

As they glided away from the safety of the dock, it was the first time in a long time that all the team members felt as though they were *in the same boat*. At that very moment, it became clear that every seat had equal value. It was odd for them. They were used to working on their own, at their own pace, not too concerned with the other people on the team. To be successful, they would have to pull together. Christine sensed a small change as they pushed off the dock together. Was it her imagination?

She hoped the rest of them felt it too—a sense of responsibility for the people around them. *Certainly they must know what that feels like,* she thought. *They have families, friends, and other responsibilities. Do they even think about their responsibility to their work team? Do they care? How do they regard one another?* These were all questions she hoped they would explore.

On the Water

On warm summer days, scores of pleasure craft can be seen traveling across Lake Union on their way to Puget Sound. Yet despite the lovely surroundings, including views of Seattle and the Space Needle, the team focused on the challenging task before them, unnerved slightly by the background sound of a seaplane taking off somewhere across the water.

The first drill they performed involved members on the port side of the boat lifting their hands while those on the other side, the starboard, pushed their hands down. Bill explained that this drill was necessary for them to figure out how to balance their own boat. However, doing the drill made the boat suddenly list all the way to one side. It was a bit frightening, and most of them thought they were going to fall into the lake. Still, they trusted Bill and continued doing what he said.

Then they switched roles, with ports raising their hands while starboards lowered theirs. They continued raising and lowering their hands, rocking the boat violently back and forth for several seconds. After a minute or two, the boat started to feel balanced and the team felt as though they had control of it.

It wasn't long before everyone realized how hard it would be for the boat to actually capsize. Bill explained that in an 8, there are eight oars spanning out over 12 feet on either side, which transforms the boat into a kind of giant water skipper. Picturing a giant water bug gave them a moment of comfort.

During the second drill they laid theirs oars parallel to the water with their arms outstretched, then slid up and down the slide to get used to moving their seats in tandem without jabbing the back of the person in front of them.

Everyone did just fine. Their confidence picked up a bit.

Real Strokes

Now the time had come for the team to take some real strokes. Bill explained that the team would start out by rowing in pairs: first, stroke and 7 seats; then, 6 and 5; 4 and 3; and 2 and bow seats. After they mastered rowing in pairs, the plan was to row by fours, then sixes, and finally all eight at the same time. Those who weren't rowing during the exercise would focus on balancing the boat to make it easier for those who were rowing.

While the first pair, Chip in 8 seat and Dave in 7 seat, was trying to learn the basic rowing stroke, the other six

teammates were helping balance the boat by keeping their oars flat on the water. Learning to take a proper stroke wasn't that hard. What *was* difficult was taking a stroke while moving forward and backward on a sliding seat. Chip was the leader, and it was up to him to set the pace. Dave had Chip in front of him and Marie right behind him with her oar flat on the water helping to balance the boat. As Dave was trying to row while moving in tandem with Chip, he also kept a sharp eye on Marie's floating oar so he wouldn't hit it and upset the balance of the boat.

It soon was clear that rowing in pairs was easier for some than it was for others. Chip and Dave started off well, though Chip went up the slide a bit too fast, which made it hard for Dave to follow him. Kim, their coxswain, who was sitting facing Chip, gave him some instant feedback. He acted on it almost immediately and it helped. The pair was rewarded with quick results. They moved the boat and it felt good.

Marie and Tim also did very well, because Marie had not only studied the rowing stroke before the event, but had also been training on a rowing machine at her health club for the past several weeks. Both of them had paid close attention during their instruction. Watching Chip and Dave go first gave them an added advantage. Again, the boat moved.

Nancy and Christine were well matched as a pair, keeping the same pace and trying their best not to over-perform and wear themselves out. Their performance was rather uneventful as the boat smoothly moved through the water without causing the balance to be upset. The boat moved at a steady pace and by now the team was getting used to the drill.

Unfortunately for Doug and Peter, by the time they were supposed to take their turn, the team was getting a little bored from having to balance the boat for such a long time. Chip started daydreaming about the fishing trip he had planned with his brother that weekend. Christine was thinking through her dinner speech, and Tim was wondering what to get his wife for her birthday.

The rest of the team was simply not paying attention. They were lost in their own thoughts, and the loss of focus took its toll. As they took their first few strokes, the boat lurched to one side and Doug screamed out, "Ahhh!" In turn, Peter stopped rowing, with his arms outstretched, frozen in mid air. Doug continued rowing and his back slammed into Peter's oar handle.

"Ouch!" Doug screamed. "Don't hit me with your oar."

"I didn't hit you," Peter replied, "You hit my oar."

Doug was confused. Since they were all facing forward, he couldn't see Peter behind him and hadn't realized that Peter had stopped rowing. As the boat came to an awkward stop, a dark cloud rolled in and the wind kicked up on the lake.

"Everything you do or don't do affects others," Bill reminded the team as he pulled up in his small motorboat. "Working in unison is imperative for maintaining balance, so you've really got to pay attention to everything that's going on around you.

"Remember, the first part of the Rowers' Code is *Always Do What's Best for the Team*. I am sure some of you are getting tired balancing the boat, but we have one more pair to go before we move forward, so let's all focus on balancing the boat so the last two rowers can have their chance to learn to row. You can do it!"

Taking Bill's words to heart, and after another few tries, the crew was finally able to get into sync, restoring balance to the boat, which made it easier for Peter and Doug, as well as everyone else, to work as a team.

Summary and Key Concepts

♦ A racing shell is engineered for one thing only—speed. At 23 inches wide, racing shells can be rather deceiving and might look very unstable. However, years of data and computer modeling have helped boat makers produce ideal shells, which are both fast and stable. Combining technology with the right team members in the right seats, sharing the load and carrying their weight, makes a team a strong force.

♦ Sometimes it's just not your turn, and, at those times, you must still focus on your team role to ensure the boat is balanced while your other teammates do their jobs.

Chapter 8

One Step Back

The exercise of rowing in pairs had given each team member a chance to learn the basic stroke with just one other person to worry about. In essence, they became four mini-teams. Now it was time for them to move on to the next level: four people rowing at a time.

"Alright, let's begin again, this time with the four stern positions: seats 8, 7, 6, and 5," Bill called out from his launch right next to the rowing shell, as a fresh breeze rippled the water and a speedboat passed well off the bow.

Feeling confident, the stern four started out rowing too fast, resulting in chaos. Oars flew all over the place, and the boat twisted in the water. It was frightening.

"Hold water!" Kim quickly shouted, calling out the command for them to stop the boat. The bow four didn't understand if she was talking to the entire team or just the stern four, and kept balancing the boat instead of helping the stern four bring it to a stop. To make things worse, the stern four couldn't remember exactly what to do to stop the boat so it took a while for them to bring it to a complete halt.

When the boat finally stopped, Kim called out, "Sit easy!" which meant everyone should keep their oars flat on the water and relax. Unfortunately, a few of them forgot about their responsibility to keep the boat balanced. Two people let go of their oars. Suddenly the craft tipped to one side. It felt as if they were going to pour right into the lake.

"Balance the boat!" Kim shouted at the top of her lungs, sounding extremely annoyed. The two people who had let go of their oars grabbed them and the rest of the team immediately put their oars on the water. Magically, they regained complete control of their boat after a few adrenalin-filled seconds.

The skies darkened overhead and Bill felt the wind from the south end of the lake pick up even more. *Is it a sign?* he wondered. He hoped not.

Regrouping

"Look, this is your boat," Kim said. "It's up to you to decide how you row it and how you balance it. I don't want to end up in the lake today. So, while we take a break, you need to be responsible for your own oar and help to keep the boat balanced. Stay focused. Whatever you do, do not let go of your oars."

Kim's annoyance was apparent to everyone. A few of them felt guilty for forgetting about their oars and upsetting the balance of the boat, even if it was just for a moment. Doug sat in amazement, realizing what had just happened. When he felt that the boat was going to tip over, in a desperate attempt to save himself, he let the team down by letting go of his oar and grabbing the side of the boat. The amazing part was that as soon as he listened to Kim and took hold of his oar once again, the boat stabilized and the entire team felt safe.

A large gust of wind blew over the lake and shook the boat. Bill started to get anxious. If the weather continued to decline, this novice crew would have a very difficult time getting the boat back into the dock. Although some of them had participated in water sports in the past, rowing was different. He hoped Kim wasn't too annoyed or worried by their lack of focus.

Kim wasn't worried. Everything from not paying attention to letting go of oars was all part of learning to row. As they sat waiting for Bill's wise words of encouragement, Kim reminisced about her first time rowing and how she did almost everything wrong. This made her smile and she felt a pang of compassion for the team.

Bill pulled up to the boat in his launch. 'How's it going, everyone?' he asked.

Christine spoke up. "I think we're doing fine, though this is harder than I originally thought. There's so much to keep track of—arms, backs, legs, rowing in tandem with the person in front of us, putting our oars in the water together, keeping our hands level, balancing the boat, and all the unfamiliar commands. It isn't easy coordinating everything at once. I just don't know what to focus on."

She couldn't have said it any better. They all agreed, even Chip and Doug.

Staying in Sync

"Ok, you sound a bit overwhelmed," Bill replied. "You need to learn about your team's bandwidth, how many processes it can handle at one time. Actually, many of the problems can be solved with proper timing. This is a good time to introduce the next point in the Rowers' Code."

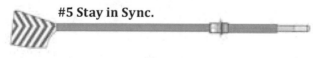

#5 Stay in Sync.

"Staying in sync is about timing and doing what's necessary to be efficient as a team, so you don't waste energy or wear yourselves out," Bill explained as his launch bobbed in the water nearby. "This means moving up and down the slide together, putting your oars in the water together, applying even pressure to the stroke, and then taking your oar out of the water together and recovering for the next stroke—all as a cohesive unit." It sounded easy as Bill talked about it, but was much harder to actually execute.

As he spoke, Bill demonstrated what each team member would be doing, taking one stroke at a time. After explaining the drill once more with some added detail, he got the stern four started. It was rocky at first, but everyone quickly grasped it.

Then it was time for the bow four to give it a try. They easily performed the drill and were quite pleased with themselves. Christine was happy because she realized being in 4 seat was a leadership position too. She was the leader of the bow four.

The team added their backs and legs to their strokes, and were rowing just fine as stern four and bow four. Kim was calling out the drill. They rowed ten strokes at a time, switching back and forth between the stern four and bow four. Being successful at this drill felt good and helped restore their confidence.

Without notice Kim called out, "in two strokes let's have stern pair and bow pair only with the powerhouse at 6, 5, 4, and 3 balancing the boat. In two—one, two—stern pair and bow pair only."

It was a bit shaky for a few seconds as the team struggled to get it together, but they pulled it off and kept rowing. They were all proud of themselves. Several grinned, including Doug, who was sweating like mad in his suit.

Just when they were feeling really confident, Kim ordered, "Okay, in two strokes let's have the stern pair and bow pair balancing the boat while 6, 5, 4, and 3 row together. In two—one, two—6, 5, 4, 3 rowing." They switched over like the gears of a finely tuned watch. Someone yelled out "Wahoo, we got it!"

The entire team was all smiles. Bill was happy too. He enjoyed seeing their hard-won success. It was evident that backing up a bit had huge returns for this team.

"Okay, it's time to start rowing all six," Bill commanded. "In two, let's have the stern six rowing arms only and bow pair balancing the boat. In two—one, two—stern six rowing, bow pair balancing."

It would have been great if the team had done exactly what he instructed. But a few of them, still excited from the last drill, ignored the arms-only direction and ran their oars right into the backs of the people in front of them.

"Ouch!" Chip screamed as the boat stopped.

"Sorry," Dave muttered. "I forgot what we were doing."

Kim jumped right in. "I didn't tell anyone to stop rowing. Let's pick it up. Arms only, stern six. Let's row."

They immediately began again, only this time some of them moved their arms too fast and some missed the water completely. "Let's focus on even hands and balancing the boat," Kim instructed. "Pace yourselves and work together. You can do it!" she shouted.

They could do it, and they did. Before long they were rowing with arms, backs, and legs, taking turns from stern six to bow six every ten strokes. It felt good—really good. Having two people balance the boat while the others rowed worked for them. It was the perfect combination of balance and power.

While Christine was focused on the task at hand, she was also pondering the lesson they had learned about taking a step back. She knew in her heart there was a deeper lesson there for her team.

Kim called for a break before they would begin trying to row all eight. At her command, the team dropped their blades sharply in the water and brought the boat to an abrupt halt. With the boat bobbing gently on the lake, they took a long water break, smiling and laughing. Soon they would face the challenge of rowing all eight at the same time. They had no idea how hard it would be.

Summary and Key Concepts

Rowers' Code:	Meaning:	Core Principle:
#5 Stay in Sync.	Timing is everything. Realizing that everything you do affects others. Knowing your bandwidth and the bandwidth of others.	Situational awareness

- ♦ Staying in sync is about timing and doing what's necessary to be efficient as a team. Staying in sync requires the perfect combination of balance and power.

- ♦ Working as a team is not always intuitive. It takes understanding and learning the right skills, and then working together to practice them and perfect them.

- ♦ You may not believe that your role, or another's role on the team, is critical to overall success, but it is. The team depends on everyone to carry their load. Everything you do or don't do affects others. Doing your part has a huge impact on the success of the team.

Chapter 9

The Sun Comes Out

During their break, Kim explained to the team members that they would have to balance the boat themselves as they rowed. They understood all too well what that meant, because now they had experienced firsthand how it became increasingly harder to balance the boat and stay in sync as more of them were added in to row during each drill. The team was understandably nervous, and they were getting tired. They had already been out on the water for more than an hour and a half.

Just as they were ready to begin this latest challenge, the sun broke through the clouds. Looking up at the sky, Kim said, "See, it's a good sign. I know some of you are nervous, but you are doing well, and I know you can do it."

Bill listened to Kim's pep talk and decided he didn't need to say anything more. She could not have said it better. The team was ready. It was time to row all eight.

Before setting off, Bill asked them if they wanted to start with arms only, adding in legs and backs later, or just begin by rowing full out. Since they were getting tired, they chose the latter.

"Are you sure?" Bill queried them. "That's not what has worked for you so far." *They don't seem to learn from their mistakes,* he thought to himself. *The idea of rowing all eight is exciting, and they want to look like the team in the video, but they don't fully realize the thought and effort that goes into it.*

"We can do it," Marie replied. "Let's go already!"

Doug shouted, "Yeah, let's go. I'm hungry!"

Doug was not only hungry. A little voice in his head was berating him for coming unprepared. He told himself that next time he would bring the appropriate clothing for the event, even if he didn't want to participate. Everyone else was silently waiting for Bill's instructions.

Doing Their Own Thing

Bill nodded to Kim. "Alright then, let's have all eight sitting ready to row," Kim said, pausing so they could get in place and she could grab hold of the gunnels. "Ready all... ROW!"

Without having anyone focus exclusively on balancing the boat, it seemed as though the vessel had a mind of its own as it violently tipped from one side to the other, water splashing everywhere. Kim shouted out at the top of her lungs, "Weigh enough! Hold water!"

They haphazardly set their oars in the water and the boat finally came to an awkward stop. Not knowing what else to do, the team sat quietly, waiting for instruction.

Bill steered his launch up to the team. "It looks like you are all doing your own thing, and it's not pretty." He shouted above a seaplane flying overhead. "When the going gets tough, you have two choices: you can work as a team and pull together, or you can do your own thing and pull apart. It's up to you."

He was right. They were all doing *their own thing* instead of working as a team, which explained why the boat was out of control. Their experiences in the boat mirrored their experiences at work.

"You need to become one boat and know what that feels like," Bill added. To most of the team, they were not one boat and had no idea what that would even feel like.

However, Nancy remembered how nice it felt when they rowed in pairs. A few times the strokes they took were so well-synchronized that it felt as though they were one person rowing instead of two. She knew exactly what Bill was talking about.

Still, the team was tired and they were getting hungry. It was time to start back to the boathouse.

Leading by Example

Things don't always happen as expected. Shortly after they started out on their adventure, the sky was overcast and the lake was calm. Now the sun was pouring down on them, but the water was getting rough. Doug began complaining about the heat.

"Well, if you weren't wearing a suit, you wouldn't be so hot," Nancy snapped at him. She was right. Doug felt guilty. He had let his team down and he knew it.

"But it *is* hot out here," Chip murmured.

"Well, maybe we should stop talking and get rowing," Marie intoned.

"I'm with you on that," said Tim.

"It may be hot and the water is getting choppy, but we need to stay focused and get this boat back into the house." Kim reminded them.

"Sit ready to row," Kim shouted. Instantly, they sat up in their seats, waiting for her next command. "And row!"

As they began rowing again, oars were flying all over the place. Bill had them stop the boat, pulled up in his launch and smiled. "This isn't going very well," he said, "I think it's time to learn the next point in the Rowers' Code."

#6 Lead by Example.

Going well? Things weren't *going* at all, though Bill's smile managed to put them at ease for a moment as they waited in earnest for their next lesson.

"I have a good third-party perspective out here in my little boat," he told the team. "I can see your entire boat, each of you, and the water ahead. You're in your boat right in the thick of things just trying to manage your own oar, so your perspective about what is really going on around you is limited."

He's right, thought Tim. *I really have no idea what anyone is doing around me. I just trust that they are doing what they should be doing, but I don't really know. I think I am doing things correctly, but I'm not sure myself.*

"Remember this morning when Angela said that everything you do affects others?" Bill asked. "Well it does. Chip is trying really hard to set the pace, for example, but Marie keeps going really fast up the slide and is pushing him, or at least making him feel pushed."

That's right, thought Chip, *I feel like someone has been pushing me the whole time we've been out here.*

"But he can't see her pushing him, he can only feel it," Bill added. "Tim is pulling his oar in high like he's rowing over a giant ball instead of a tabletop and that's pushing Christine's oar into her lap."

Everyone agreed. Bill was right again.

"In the back of the boat, you two guys are always late," Bill continued. "You're late up the slide and late with your oars. Late, late, late. It's making the boat lurch, especially when you both lean to one side."

Chip wanted to substitute "lazy" for "late," but he kept that thought to himself. Peter wanted to sink under his seat. He had been trying to be invisible all morning, and now it sounded like Bill thought he was a slacker. Bill saw the look on Peter's face and thought he embarrassed him a bit.

Bill gave Kim the nod to get the team rowing. "Let's have all eight sitting ready to row. Ready all...ROW!" Kim yelled out.

Summary and Key Concepts

Rowers' Code:	Meaning:	Core Principle:
#6 Lead by Example.	Trusting in yourself and others. Sharing leadership responsibility.	Trust

♦ As much as we would all like to believe that people follow our vision, in reality people follow people. For words to hit home with people and make a difference, behavior has to align. It starts with you.

♦ Make small adjustments and focus on doing the right things, because even small changes have an exponential affect on the team.

Chapter 10

A Final Push

"I'm not trying to be overly hard on any of you," Bill told the team, "but you need to get it together to get this boat back into the boathouse."

As Christine listened to Bill talk, she started thinking about the work that lay ahead. From what their former boss had told her and what she was experiencing on the water with them, it seemed that when the going got tough, her team pulled apart. She kept thinking that her biggest challenge would be to get her team to pull together and work as one.

"Let me give you a few more tips," Bill added. "Focus your hands at a single point on the back of the person in front of you and aim for that spot every time you reach forward to take a stroke. That will keep your hands even and help balance the boat. Go slow up the slide and stay together. Put your oars in the water together and take them out together. Set an example for the person behind you to follow. You can do it."

There was no doubt that rowing as a team was a lot harder than most of them had thought. Tim and Nancy imagined the team rowing in perfect synchronicity. In their imaginations, this team looked like an awesome championship rowing crew. But that wasn't reality.

While Tim and Nancy were daydreaming, the rest of them wondered how they would ever pull it together enough to get back to the boathouse. Bill's instruction was helping them, but they still had to row the boat themselves. No matter how well any of them thought they were rowing, the boat seemed to take on a life of its own.

What Bill said was true—it wasn't pretty. They were so engrossed in their own individual performance that they couldn't even feel the other people around them. For some, having to coordinate so many things at the same time was just overwhelming. It felt like the blind leading the blind. They were all tired and had no idea if they were even rowing correctly. But they were coming to the realization that if they didn't work together, their boat was going nowhere.

An Oar in the Back

The team waited for Bill's command to start rowing. It was time for them to pull it together. Bill gave Kim the signal to get the boat moving.

"Ok, let's sit ready to row...and row!" Kim commanded.

Chip was exhausted from leading the team. With the hot sun beating down on him and water swirling all around the boat, Chip could hardly hold on to his oar. Convinced that they were going to capsize, he gripped his oar even harder, sweat running down his forehead and dripping into his eyes. The sweat burned as he tried to blink it away, too afraid to let go of his oar to wipe his brow. He was trying his best to concentrate and do a good job, but the boat was rocking violently back and forth. He felt nauseous and thought he was going to throw up.

Just as he finally took a clean stroke, Dave jabbed him again in the back with his oar. As pain shot up his spine, Chip realized how angry he was. He didn't want to be angry, but by this time Dave had stabbed him in the back so many times that Chip started thinking it was on purpose. He shook his head in frustration, centered himself, and took another stroke.

The boat started to move forward as Chip prepared himself for it to lunge even more violently than before. He heard the coach shouting out something that was unintelligible. He strained to hear, but a passing motor boat drowned out Bill's cries and he could only hear the voice inside his head telling him to hang on, that it would all be over soon.

Dave felt horrible. He didn't mean to jab Chip in the back, but he was so focused on his own oar that he couldn't even see in front of him. He tried to say something, to apologize, when the coach yelled out, "No talking in the boat, stay focused and keep your eyes on the person in front of you," He decided to apologize to Chip when they returned to the dock.

"Weigh enough, hold water!" Kim shouted abruptly.

At her command, the team stopped rowing and set their blades cleanly in the water. The boat stopped immediately, a few feet from the dock.

Back at the Dock

Resting easy at last, with the dock just a few inches from their reach, most of the group was pleased with how well they performed as a team. Not more than a few hours ago they were learning the parts of the boat and rowing terminology. Now they could handle the commands their coach and coxswain cried out.

Sitting at the dock, Chip shook his head again and everything seemed to return to normal. *Wow, that was some experience,* he thought to himself.

Dave was still feeling embarrassed about hitting Chip in the back with his oar. After all, he'd smacked Chip so many times that he'd lost count. After they were all up and out of the boat, standing safely on the dock, Dave grimaced, remembering a meeting the week before in which he was accused of backstabbing. *Great,* he thought, failing to see any humor or irony in what had happened. *Now everyone thinks I am a backstabber, in the boat and at work. I get so focused on what I am doing, that I don't even see the people around me.*

They all had a thousand thoughts running through their heads. But now wasn't the time for that. They still had to focus together on getting the 8 back into the boathouse, a challenge that would take the concerted effort of every team member working together to get the boat up the ramp and back inside.

And they did it, though it wasn't easy and they were tired. Kim gave them clear directions, and every team member worked together. Before they knew it, they were up the ramp and carrying it into the boathouse.

Once the boat was back in its spot, everyone cheered. They had learned so much about themselves and each other during the rowing exercise. Although they shared a communal feeling of victory, it was evident that they had a lot to learn about working together as a team. They all knew it, too. The task of setting their own "work boat" would be even harder than their accomplishment out on the water.

Summary and Key Concepts

♦ To master teamwork, you must constantly work together, keeping sight of the big goal and your own part in it. The challenge is to be in the seat that maximizes the strengths of the entire team, even as your team changes.

Chapter 11

Everything Stays in the Boat

As they ate lunch, the team was treated to a slide show made up of pictures and video clips Angela took of them rowing. Normally, they would have been answering e-mail and focusing on lunch, but on this occasion they were captivated by the images of themselves propelling the boat forward, playing on a screen at the front of the room.

Some of the footage was great, some not so great, and at times it was funny—they could easily see how Bill's descriptions fit them. In some of the pictures the boat was so unbalanced and they were so out of sync that it looked like they were about to capsize. For the most part, though, it did appear to work, and in the majority of the photos they actually looked like a team.

Rowing is the perfect teamwork metaphor, Dave realized. *It was about teamwork in the boat, with everyone doing their part.* It had been so difficult to get everyone coordinated and in sync. From the start, there were a few of them who deep down inside weren't sure they would actually be able to do it. But they had succeeded. They had all pulled together, powering up the Olympic-style shell that was 60 feet long and only a couple feet wide.

I have to get these pictures to show to my friends, thought Nancy.

I can't wait to show my picture to Sue and the kids, Tim thought to himself. *They won't believe it.* For a moment Tim was happy and forgot all about the problems he was having at work.

Everyone, in fact, was thinking about showing the pictures to their families and friends. While they ate, they kept staring at the slide show while smiling to themselves.

Angela waited until they finished eating and then stood at the front of the room. "Before we continue, I'd like to introduce the final point in the Rowers' Code:

#7 Keep Everything in the Boat.

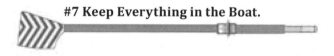

"This means that what happens in this room, stays in this room, and what happens in this team, stays in this team. Can we all agree?" She looked around the room. "Okay, if you agree, come stand in a circle, put your hands together in the middle, and say so." They all stood, moved into a tight circle, joined their hands in the middle and shouted, "I agree!"

Teamwork Takes Practice

"Jim Deitz, a great rowing coach, once said, 'Rowing is a sport for dreamers. As long as you put in the work, you can own the dream. When the work stops, the dream disappears,'" Angela said. "Well, I've modified it a bit. Here's my version: 'Rowing is a sport for dreamers. As long as you put in the *team*work, you can own the dream. When the *team*work stops, the dream disappears.' It's true. It takes constant teamwork to make big things happen."

Peter raised his hand. "Yes, Peter?" Angela asked, "Do you have something you want to say?"

"I have a question."

"Go ahead."

"I was wondering why you keep saying it takes constant work. What do you mean by that? What is the work you're referring to?"

"That's a good question," she answered. "What I mean is that it takes purposeful behavior to work as a team and live by the Rowers' Code—just like when you were learning to row. It looked easy, but when you tried it yourselves, you had to focus on doing the right things in tandem with everyone around you. It doesn't come naturally. Teamwork is the same. It's a skill that you have to learn, and then practice, practice, practice until it's second nature. You have to make a focused effort or it won't happen. The rowers you saw in the video earlier today, and the ones who rowed by your boat flawlessly, have been practicing for years. Not only do they know how to row well, they know how to row well together. There's a big difference."

"So how do we learn to do that?"

"That's what I am here to teach you. By agreeing to keep everything in the boat, you've already taken the first step towards making this work. But that's not all of it. There's more."

Talking Outside of the Boat

"Keeping everything in the boat not only means that you don't talk outside of your team, but it also means that if you have an issue with someone on this team, you go directly to that person and not to someone else. This point in the Rowers' Code is one of the most important."

Tim's face turned red. *Fat chance*, he thought, *Not on this team. Doug can't keep anything in the boat.* Angela saw the look on his face and asked him if he would like to say something. He didn't know if he should bring it up or not, but he answered her. "In my opinion, we haven't been very good at it. No one wants to be accountable or even acknowledge when we don't keep things in our own boat. It's become second nature for us to have the opposite behavior."

"Wait just a minute..." interrupted Chip.

"Chip, let him finish," Angela said. "Go ahead Tim."

"Well, I don't want to go into all the details. Christine wasn't even here when it happened the last time. But let's just say it involved someone on the team talking outside of the boat. And it really cost us. Maybe we should just drop it and move ahead. I shouldn't have brought it up."

"But, you just said that no one wanted to acknowledge it, right?" Angela asked.

"Yes, but..." Tim hesitated.

"But nothing," Angela replied. "The reason I am bringing this point up now is because it's the number-one killer of teams. I want to make sure we all agree because talking outside of the boat breaks down trust. It destroys teams and careers. If you are on a team, you owe it to your teammates to keep everything in the boat."

Summary and Key Concepts

Rowers' Code:	Meaning:	Core Principle:
#7 Keep Everything in the Boat.	Communicating clearly and honestly with your teammates.	Integrity and ownership

♦ It takes purposeful behavior to work as a team and live by the Rowers' Code.

♦ Working as a team is not always intuitive It takes knowing and understanding the skills you are learning and then working together to practice them and perfect them.

♦ Talking outside of the boat is the number-one killer of teams. It destroys trust. If you have an issue with someone on your team, go directly to that person and not to someone else.

Chapter 12

Talk Is Cheap

The discussion about accountability and keeping everything in the boat resonated all too strongly for Tim. He knew exactly what Angela was talking about. The truth was that he felt his career was at risk because of an incident that had happened recently at work. Just talking about it replaced all the joy he felt from rowing with the fear of losing his job. He was terrified. He sat there paralyzed wishing he never said a word.

"But what if it doesn't involve you?" asked Marie.

"If you are aware of something that involves a team-mate, then it does involve you," replied Angela.

"But, it wasn't my problem. I really had nothing to do with it. They didn't need one more person getting in the middle of it to make things more complicated."

"Did it affect your team?" Angela asked.

"Yes," answered Marie.

"Did you know about it?"

"Yes," Marie replied again.

"After you knew about it, and especially after you were aware that it affected your team, it was definitely your responsibility to do something. It was the responsibility of anyone on the team who knew about it to do something. Ownership doesn't stop at keeping things in the boat yourself. That's where it starts. It's up to everyone on the team to maintain it."

"But you can only control your own behavior," Marie offered.

"Yes Marie, that's true. However, if you know someone is talking outside of the boat and you don't say something, not speaking up makes you just as guilty as the person who did it. It's just like when you were in the boat today. You can't hold on to someone else's oar and row for him. But, if you know something isn't working you can point it out and get help with it. It's your responsibility to do that for your team. Everyone on the team owns the boat. Everyone is responsible."

Troubled Waters

Most of the team felt guilty about what had happened with Tim, especially the ones who knew what was going on and did nothing about it. Tim was a great guy, a hard worker who cared about his work and his team. He always made himself available when others needed help, dropping what he was doing to pitch in and lend a hand. As times he even let them borrow resources to meet tough deadlines and milestones. It really wasn't fair to him that the situation got out of hand and rumors started to fly—not fair at all.

Doug was starting to get nervous. He knew that he was the one Tim was referring to. He was the one who talked outside of the boat, and everyone knew it. *Please let this die,* he thought.

"Does anyone have anything else they want to add?" asked Angela. They all sat in silence for a moment.

Then Christine spoke up, "I don't really know what happened, but I do know this. What Angela is saying is true: it boils down to trust. If we want to do great things together, we have to trust one another."

"That's true." said Angela. "Most people who do nothing think that doing something won't help. It comes from a lack of belief in their own ability to influence others positively. Let me put it this way: If you thought you could make a difference, would you? Or, are you just lazy and don't want to make the effort?

"I can tell you from experience that making the effort up front to create a positive work culture is worth it. I'll bet you didn't all start at your present company on the same day. Instead you all come from different backgrounds and different corporate and team cultures. Based on the cultural variation in any group of diverse people, you can't possibly assume that each person will behave the same in every situation."

"I guess it all depends on the person's intentions," Peter added. "I don't know everyone yet, so I assume you all have good intentions, but like I said, I don't really know you yet."

"Peter's right. Intentions have a lot to do with behavior," said Angela. "And, I don't think you really know someone until you know how they react in a challenging situation. It's easy to display good behavior when things are going well, but you see who someone really is when there are troubled waters and the going gets tough.

"This works the same for most teams. When teams face difficult times, if they are solid, they will back each other up and things will stabilize. If not, the team will display behavior that will ultimately pull them apart. It's not easy. Good behavior has to be purposeful and you have to practice it every day."

They all knew what she was talking about from their rowing experience. At one point, when the going got tough, they all started doing their own thing and that made it that much worse. When they focused their energy on working together instead of doing their own thing or fighting each other, they got back in sync and it wasn't so hard after all.

Misunderstandings Happen

Angela decided it was a good time for everyone to take a break.

Doug was relieved. He was hoping the group would drop the "talking outside of the boat" discussion and move on. He didn't want his new boss to know the details of what had happened.

It was quite innocent really. At the end of the last quarter Doug had gone to lunch with some friends from college who worked in another division. Of course his friends asked him how things were going, and he explained that his boss of several years decided to take a job in another division. He also told them he wasn't sure which direction his team would be headed; that the team wasn't sure of its future IT needs, specifically what kind of budget they would need or what they should really focus on.

He also complained a bit about Chip challenging him and others in meetings. It came across the wrong way and it backfired. One of guys he thought was his friend twisted what Doug had said. His "friend" made it sound as though IT had lost their focus, Tim couldn't manage his budget, and that there was a general lack of direction on the team.

The story got out of hand. With talk about cutting resources, the team was getting pressure to severely trim the IT budget. Rumors were flying everywhere, especially those about some people being let go because they weren't able to manage their departments or their budgets. Doug and especially Tim were hoping it would blow over after some time passed. But it wasn't blowing over. It seemed as though everyone in the company was becoming more and more focused on it. And no one on the team felt that they were in a position to do anything about it.

During the break, Christine pulled Angela aside and asked her if they should continue the discussion or let it go for now. Angela suggested that they ask the team if they were ready to move on. Christine agreed that it should be up to the team to decide.

◆◆◆

When they returned from the break, Angela began by saying, "Let's decide if we are ready to move on." Doug smiled. Maybe he would get out of discussing it after all. Angela continued, "I'd like to see a thumbs-up for everyone who agrees with moving forward, a thumbs-down for anyone who disagrees, and a thumb to the side for anyone who is not sure." Almost everyone wanted to move on, so thumbs went up all around the room, except for Peter, who had one more question he wanted to ask.

"Is there ever a time when it's okay to go outside of the boat?" Peter asked.

"No," Angela answered. "Even if you have tried your best to work something out, going to talk to people outside your own boat is not acceptable. What *is* acceptable though is to agree as a team that you will bring someone else in to help you."

"Isn't that the same thing?" Peter asked.

"No," Angela replied. "It's not the same. When you bring someone in it's at the request of the team, not an individual, and the person you bring in has a responsibility to the entire team. When a team member goes outside the boat, there is no responsibility to the team on the part of the person he or she goes to. Going outside the boat often backfires for this very reason. The individual who goes outside the team often comes off as complaining. Sometimes the person he talks to doesn't even know or may not believe he is going to the outside person to get help. The right information might not get disclosed, it might get distorted or conveyed the wrong way—all kinds of things can happen. Mostly though, misunderstandings occur, rumors start, and people get hurt."

In this case, people did get hurt, and it wasn't over yet. What she was talking about was real, especially for Tim.

Summary and Key Concepts

♦ In times of calm waters, the skills of each team are not always apparent. It's when rough water hits that a highly skilled crew team uses their experience and skills to pull ahead of the competition.

♦ When a team member makes a mistake, the reaction of the team is critical to either building up or breaking down trust. Supporting behavior builds trust and attacking behavior destroys it. Team members must feel safe and secure within their team so that they can be open about their mistakes and ask for help in doing a better job.

♦ Everyone on the team owns "the boat" and is responsible for what happens. It is each member's responsibility to take action to improve the performance of the team.

Chapter 13

The Challenge

Trying to be part of the discussion, Dave asked, "Don't you think it comes down to having the right people on the bus?" Dave was thinking about recent talk he heard in the company about that concept. He wanted to look as though he was in the know about current business themes.

"The right people on the bus?" Angela questioned. "What do you mean by that?"

"You know, if we have the right people on the bus, then these things—these misunderstandings—wouldn't happen. We all ride along in harmony." Dave replied, feeling very pleased with himself.

In a way, a few of them agreed with Dave. With all the changes they had been through the last several months and rumors of more cuts, some of the team members were acting as though they were on a kind of a bus, riding around, waiting for the next thing to happen. And, now they had a new bus driver, Christine.

Christine didn't want to let this opportunity pass. She stood up and addressed the team. "Dave, I'm glad you said that about having the right people on the bus. One of the reasons I picked rowing—instead of hiking or playing golf—is that rowing requires everyone to participate. With the challenges we face, I need everyone to now get off the bus and into the boat. I need everyone rowing together in the same direction" She paused as she looked out at them, wondering if they were listening, if they were still engaged, and hoping they understood her.

"With the economy, competition, and challenges we face, our company is relying on us to get the boat moving in the right direction. We can't wait for someone else to do that. *We* have to do it. We own our boat and I expect each of you to own your seat and your oar. I can't stress it enough," she said.

"As we face these new challenges, I feel as though we are venturing out onto the unchartered waters of change, where we will need everyone to participate and power up the boat. You have all been on the bus. Now it's time for you to get off the bus, get in the boat, and row like you've never rowed before." She paused while she looked out at them to see if they were still with her. They were.

The Challenge

Peter did think about it. He recalled the times when he had been on teams that had many bus riders—people who got recruited and then did next to nothing, or people who said they would pitch in and instead pitched a fit whenever there was hard work to do. He understood exactly what Christine was talking about.

Angela picked up Christine's thread from there, explaining that in the boat, everyone understands his or her role and its importance to the team. Everyone is responsible for their own oar and works together to propel the boat in the right direction. The team understands that what they do and don't do has a huge impact on their success."

The analogies Christine and Angela made of the bus and boat were good ones. Everyone understood them. They especially hit home with Christine. Just two weeks before, her boss had been telling her the exact words, "you have to get the right people on the bus." But, Angela was right. Considering the challenges in front of them, there was no bus—not where they were going. Christine would have to talk to her boss and her peers. They had good intentions and wanted to do great things, but they were using the wrong words when they said they had to get the right people on the bus.

Christine again took the lead. "The question I want you to ask yourself is, Do I want to be a bus rider or a rower? Rowing isn't for everyone. Are you up to the challenge?" she asked. "Are your direct reports up to the challenge?"

Christine looked around the room. She wasn't sure what she saw in their eyes. Some of them nodded yes to her, looking as though they agreed and wanted to be rowers. Some of them looked at her as if she must not trust them and was questioning them. Some of them looked as though she had just punched them in the gut. How would she get across to them? How would they work together to turn bus riders into rowers?

While Christine and Angela were addressing the group, some of them realized that for the past several months they had been acting like bus riders—happy to be on the bus, but waiting for someone to lead them around until things stabilized and the economy improved. That wouldn't work. Christine made it very clear that she was not going to be their bus driver. The company needed rowers, not bus riders. They needed to be the change they envisioned. Grabbing hold of their oars and rowing together with all their might to propel their boat to victory would be the key to success.

A New Way of Behaving

Chip sat there looking up at Christine with a new appreciation for her leadership. She was right. He thought back to what Angela had said at the beginning of the day—that the experience would be new to them, like none they had experienced before. It was true. No one had ever challenged them this way. Usually the offsite meetings involved hiking, golfing, or bowling. They were often more of a social activity than a real team workshop such as they were having now. Christine was serious, and it was good for them.

Well, I'm certainly not a bus rider, Chip thought. *I am a rower. But, I row more in my own boat than the team boat.* He felt a little bad about it. In the past he thought he was helping lead the team. Now he wasn't so sure. Maybe instead he was a bit overbearing. Maybe at times he upset the balance of the boat. When they were out on the water balance had so much to do with being able to row as a team.

The rowing experience gave them instant feedback. It was amazing how quickly the boat slowed down or stopped as soon as the balance got upset. Normally at this point in a meeting, Chip would have spoken up to tell everyone what he thought. This time he was quiet. He wanted to think about it for a while. He not only thought about his own work, but also that of his direct reports, and wondered if they were up to the challenge.

Christine sat down and waited to see if anyone would say anything. When no one spoke for a few moments, Angela broke the silence. "You are all very quiet. What are you thinking?" she asked.

Tim spoke up. "You're right about the boat analogy. It's easy to understand. And it's true. Our challenges are daunting. We can't be successful unless we all work together. For me, it's a new way of thinking and a new way of behaving."

"You're right, Tim," Angela replied. It is a new way of behaving. It's a new level of intensity."

Yep, from comatose to alive and moving, Marie thought to herself. She had already been on several teams in which it felt as though the majority of the work was done by a few of the people. There were the shining stars and there were the slackers. She liked the rowing analogy. It painted a positive mental image of everyone working together. She spoke up. "I understand how we need rowers to meet our challenges, that just getting the right people on the bus won't do it. So how do we create a rower's culture?"

"That's a great question, Marie," Angela answered. "It starts at the top of the organization. Remember # 6 in the Rowers' Code, Lead by Example? It all starts with you. As a leadership team you have to hold yourselves to the same standards you expect others to live by. I try asking myself every day if the behavior I display is how I want others to act. It's a good way to check your own behavior."

Christine was proud of Marie for speaking up and asking such an important question. Marie was young, true, but she was also smart and not afraid to take risks.

Summary and Key Concepts

♦ Team success requires a rowing mentality: each person knows her roles and responsibilities, understands her importance to the success of the team, and is an active participant in producing optimal results.

♦ Change starts with leaders living the values and behaviors they would like to foster within the organization. Be present, engage your employees, and teach them how to get in the boat and row.

Chapter 14

Glimmer of Hope

Angela continued the team discussion. "Let's do an exercise that I think will help us understand a bit more where we are right now. What I want you to do is draw a picture of the current state of your team using a boat or boats. After everyone draws their pictures, we'll share them with the rest of the team."

Doug quickly started drawing and finished before everyone else on the team. His drawing had several boats in it, each going in different directions with all kinds of obstacles floating in the water around them. A few of the other drawings were similar, showing a dark sky, waves hitting the boat, and empty seats.

Chip took much longer than everyone else to finish his drawing. He was a good artist and his drawing was full of detail. His showed the team in one boat. It was dark, and there was a big wave crashing down on them.

A shark was circling the boat. There was also a small boat in the distance with a life ring attached to it. Several people were piled into the middle seats.

"Who is that?" asked Nancy, pointing to the small boat in the distance with the life ring.

"It's Christine coming to save us," answered Chip. Christine overheard him and she wondered if he had paid attention to what she just said. It felt great. Chip had finally put her in the leadership role.

Chip loved the exercise. It was his chance to show Christine that he believed in her. He felt guilty most of the morning because of the way it must have looked when he pushed his way into the leadership seat. It wasn't until Angela shared the fourth point in the Rowers' Code with them, Balance the Boat, that he realized he should have let Christine lead their team in the boat. By the time he realized it, it was a little too late. He was embarrassed. Hoping no one noticed, he thought it was better not to call attention to it. Now he realized how easy it could have been to say just something right away and reset the boat.

When Angela asked them to share their pictures, Chip jumped at the chance to go first.

"I see you only have six people in the boat," questioned Tim. "Why is that?"

"Well, I don't think we have the right mix of people in our boat, and some people aren't in the right seats," Chip answered rather matter-of-factly. Tim's face turned red.

Ouch, thought Nancy. *Nothing like kicking people out of the boat the first chance you get.*

Marie was glad he said it. *It's about time someone says what they really think,* she thought, *even if it's hard to take.*

Christine waited to see what the others would say.

Tim sank down in his seat. He was afraid that he was one of the people Chip cut from the boat. Tim was worried about losing his job. His insecurity made him take Chip's drawing the wrong way. *I guess I shouldn't have asked. My seat is possibly one of the empty ones,* he thought.

Angela waited. No one spoke. She realized they had a common problem that most teams have: that of not being able to bring up sensitive topics or contend issues without the conversation coming to a halt or going south. She wanted to hear what the other team members had to say about their drawings and she wanted to test her theory, so she asked them to continue going around the room, sharing what they drew.

The Gift

After seeing all the drawings, and hearing the team's comments, questions, and answers, Angela knew it was time to revisit the Rowers' Code and address their issues. She began, "The best teams are ones that create a safe environment for team members to bring up issues and deal with them as a team, without fear of being criticized. What I have been observing today is that you are afraid of speaking up and having real conversations about things that really matter. In my mind, it means that you get more value out of sweeping things under the rug than dealing with them. Is it true? Are you really getting value out of not dealing with things?"

Chip spoke first. As soon as the first word left his mouth he realized he was dominating the conversation again. But, he thought what he had to say was important. "No, we aren't getting any real value out of it, but we don't really know how to deal with some of the issues. Sometimes, dealing with our issues hurts each other's feelings and causes even more problems. We've had some issues so long that they just seem like they are part of our boat."

No one else wanted to be the one to say more. The room became uncomfortably silent. Marie rolled her eyes. Chip had said it all, just like he usually did before anyone else got a chance.

"I know your problem," Angela exclaimed. With that she reached into her bag and pulled out a small box. "I want everyone to line up in the front of the room in the order you were in the boat. Call out your number when you are ready, just like you did when you rowed, and I'll put something in your hand. I don't want you to open your hand and look at it until I tell you because we will open our hands together."

They all lined up and called out their numbers when they were ready.

Angela smiled. This part of her job was always great fun.

Angela placed something small in each person's hand, and they closed their fingers around it. When everyone had the mystery gift, Angela instructed them to open their hands.

In each person's hand was a tiny, yellow rubber chicken, about 1.5 inches tall. Everyone laughed, standing there looking at their tiny yellow rubber chickens, while they waited for Angela to continue.

"This is a reminder to not be a chicken. The next time you are in a situation in which you are not sure if you should say something or not, get out your chicken and ask yourself, Do I want to make a difference or do I want to be a chicken? Weigh the cost of action, but also weigh the cost of inaction. It's up to you. It's your boat."

They all liked their chickens, except for Chip and Doug. Chip thought to himself that he was never a chicken and couldn't understand why he would ever need reminding. Doug thought it was just plain stupid to give someone a rubber chicken. He started daydreaming of how he would flick it out of his window that night, but then he realized he had several things he was afraid of himself. Maybe the chicken wasn't such a stupid idea after all. He would decide the fate of his chicken later.

Angela continued, "Don't worry, the rubber chicken isn't all I'm going to give you. I'll also give you some other tools to help you work through your challenges in a positive way." She had gotten their curiosity going. She gave them a glimmer of hope. What did she know that they didn't? What tools did she have?

It was time for a break. Everyone was looking forward to the next part of the workshop.

Summary and Key Concepts

♦ The best teams and meetings are those in which the participants foster healthy debates. This can be difficult, especially when individuals have a high personal investment in the topic, and it will be given lots of exposure in the company. Being skillful at working through issues requires communicating openly and honestly, actively listening to one another and seeking to understand. It requires that you put personalities aside and focus on issues and opportunities.

♦ Don't be a chicken. Ken Blanchard wrote, "Wisdom is knowing what to do next; virtue is doing it." Courage gives reality to all of your other values by taking action, even in the face of fear.

Chapter 15

No Whining in the Boat

During the break Marie saw Nancy standing outside and decided to join her for some fresh air.

"Hi."

"Oh, hi Marie, how's it going?"

"It's going okay. I don't know about this team though."

"What do you mean?" asked Nancy.

"I'm not sure it's the right team for me."

"Why do you say that?" Nancy prodded.

"Well, it seems like people are afraid to speak up and say how they feel, Chip is a bully, and I'm probably too impatient to stay around and wait for things to change. I want so much in life.

"My dad always told me to look out for myself and to be number one; that if I didn't look out for myself, no one else would. I don't feel like I am number one, though. I have a friend, Renee, for whom everything seems to work. She has a great executive job, she jet-sets around the world, and things always work out for her. I want to be just like she is—successful. I have been waiting for things to really change, and sometimes I don't think things will change on this team."

Nancy replied, "I guess if you expect things to change while you stand on the sideline, then you are right—maybe it's not the right team for you. But, if you want to be part of the solution and help make change happen, stick it out. That's what I am going to do."

"You are?" Marie asked.

"Yes, I am." Nancy nodded and looked at Marie, smiling. "I want to be a rower, who takes hold of her oar and powers up the boat. And, you know what, Marie?"

"What?"

"I could use your help, that's what. You are very bright and full of energy. I am sure if you propel your energy in the right direction, you'll go far, and our team will too. I just have a gut feeling about it."

Nancy's words of confidence worked wonders with Marie, who smiled back at Nancy and said, "Maybe Angela should add an 8th point in the Rowers' Code."

"And what would that be?" Nancy inquired.

"No whining in the boat," Marie answered jokingly.

They both laughed. As Nancy looked at Marie she saw the younger version of herself—an impatient girl with high expectations of both herself and her peers. Nancy remembered her own father, who told her almost the exact same words as Marie's dad. She wondered if all dads told their daughters to look out for themselves because no one else would.

Nancy was the one everyone else relied on. However, Nancy didn't feel she could rely on others, especially at work. More often than not, she felt let down by her peers. They didn't seem to do what they promised and didn't seem to care when they let her down.

Sometimes it took more effort than she felt it was worth to try to get her coworkers back on track during a project. She would end up doing the work herself, which took its toll, wearing her out and ultimately causing her to feel as though she wasn't performing as well as she could.

The day's activities, however, gave her hope. Not only were they able to pull together out on the water, but in their follow-up discussions, it seemed like her coworkers were finally examining the team's problems and considering what to do about them.

Marie looked at Nancy, who seemed to be deep in thought. She was happy Nancy said she needed her. Nancy was smart and had a good reputation throughout the company. Marie could definitely learn a great deal from her.

They both smiled at each other and went back inside.

Summary and Key Concepts

♦ Playing the "ain't it awful" game through complaining about one's circumstances does not help the situation. This is not to say that we should avoid confronting problems and discussing them, but employees should bring up issues with the goal of *solving* problems. In Jon Gordon's book *The No Complaining Rule*, he suggests offering one or two solutions along with any complaint that is aired. If you see an area in your team that could be improved, and you want to make a difference, don't just complain; join with others to do something about it.

Chapter 16

Window of Opportunity

There were only a couple of hours remaining before it was time to wrap it up for the day. The team had to make the most out of the opportunities the day afforded them.

Angela began, "For the next exercise, you will take a self quiz, then split up into pairs to discuss some of your own behaviors regarding the points of the Rower's Code that we've introduced. For each point in the Rowers' Code, you'll discuss one behavior you have recently displayed that was positive and one that was negative. When you come back to the room, you'll share one positive behavior and one negative behavior with the team."

"Do you mean that we all cover every point in the Code?" Christine asked.

"No, we don't have enough time to share that much information as a group," Angela replied. "Everyone will share just one positive behavior and one negative behavior total. Here's an example using two separate points in the Rowers' Code, Carry Your Load and Balance the Boat. My negative Carry Your Load behavior is when I was working on a project with Kim and knew I couldn't make the commitments I had agreed to; I didn't forewarn her as soon as I knew it. She always came to our status meetings with her items completed, prepared to move forward, while I kept making excuses and moving the timeline. My positive Balance the Boat behavior was that I realized I was trying to juggle too much in my life. When I was recently asked to be on another committee, I said no, knowing that I couldn't meet their expectations, even though it was something I really felt I needed to be part of and wanted to do.

"So, there is an example for you. Does everyone understand what you are supposed to do?" she asked. Everyone nodded. "Okay, take the self quiz, score them, then split up into these pairs: Chip and Peter, Dave and Doug, Marie and Nancy, and Christine and Tim. Go ahead and find a quiet place where you can talk and come back in 30 minutes."

"Do you want us to share our scores from the self quiz with each other?" Nancy asked.

"No, it's not necessary. It's for your eyes only, so you can see where your strengths are and where you need improvement," Angela answered.

Self-Assessment Questions: Pick one response per question.	Strongly Agree (6)	Agree (5)	Slightly Agree (4)	Slightly Disagree (3)	Disagree (2)	Strongly Disagree (1)
1. I put the interests of the team in front of my own goals and ambitions.						
2. I consistently behave in ways that show my commitment to the team.						
3. When a decision is made, I show support by my proactive actions.						
4. I feel we have the right mix of people on our team to meet our goals.						
5. I value unique differences in my teammates and acknowledge their strengths.						
6. I understand the importance of how my individual performance relates to team success.						

7. I hold myself and my teammates accountable.						
8. I discuss team performance openly and honestly with my teammates.						
9. I inform others well in advance if I cannot keep a commitment or perform as expected.						
10. I have a clear understanding of the goals of the company.						
11. I have reasonable and achievable goals.						
12. I understand what I am personally expected to do to reach the goals of the team.						
13. I am good at prioritizing what I need to focus on.						

14. I help out my teammates, sometimes dropping what I am doing or reassigning resources.						
15. I am a master of great timing, considering others and how my actions affect them.						
16. I feel our leaders value my perspective and actively seek it out.						
17. I play an active role in decision-making.						
18. I feel I have a commitment to integrity and ethical practices.						
19. I communicate openly and honestly with my teammates.						

20. I value clarity of communication, asking my teammates for confirmation to make sure we understand each other.						
21. When there are issues, I go directly to my teammates instead of going outside the team to vent or gain support.						
Total for each column (x)						
Multiply by the weighted value (y)	X6	X5	X4	X3	X2	X1
Grand Total (x) x (y) 21–53: You do not work well with your team. 54–95: Sometimes you work well with your team. 96–126: You work well with your team.						

Pairing Up

Dave was upset by Angela's announcement. For some reason, he thought he would be paired with Chip. After they got back to the dock, he couldn't find an opportunity to talk to Chip in order to explain his behavior the prior week, when Chip thought he backstabbed him. He was hoping he would get his chance now, but that wasn't happening.

He hesitated for a moment right after Angela announced the pairs, thinking he could ask to swap partners. Then he stopped himself. His gut told him to let Angela be in charge. Somehow he would find time to talk to Chip that evening before dinner. Besides, Doug was okay. Yes, he could be a real pain, but he did hold his own at work and his numbers always made them look good.

Chip was furious. He didn't want to pair up with Peter because he was the new guy, and what did new guys know anyhow? Chip often got the new guy when they did break-out sessions and brainstorming activities.

What Chip didn't know was that his teammates often asked their leader to pair them with anyone but him. They thought he was overbearing, dominating conversations and not letting them get a word in. However, that was not the case this time. It was merely by chance that Peter and Chip were paired up.

Peter was actually happy with the match. He found Chip's leadership style intriguing. Peter wondered what Chip really felt he had to gain by constantly cutting off his peers. He couldn't wait to hear what Chip would have to say now and to see if he was even remotely interested in what Peter could contribute to the conversation.

Marie and Nancy were both happy to be paired up. The more Nancy got to know Marie, the more she liked her. Nancy saw huge amounts of potential in Marie. Marie liked Nancy's communication skills, positive attitude, and her way of making things sound so logical. Nancy asked good questions and listened to Marie when she answered. They were the perfect match for this exercise and were looking forward to it.

Christine was glad she was paired with Tim. She had been meaning to talk to him about the incident that was wreaking havoc, but wanted to collect as many facts as she could before having the discussion. Maybe she would get a chance to say something to him. If not, she would try to talk to him before dinner that evening.

Tim, on the other hand, was nervous when Angela called out his name with Christine's. He was worried his job was in jeopardy and that his new boss didn't know what really happened. Tim felt as though he was going to throw up. Should he say something? Should he avoid it? Maybe he should have approached her before the event so he could clear the air. Maybe he should stick up for himself and say something now. He guessed that if she had wanted to fire him, she would have done it already. Maybe this event was her chance to get to know him. Maybe she was making the decision right now. What would he do?

After everyone finished taking the self-quiz, it was time to pair off and discuss their behavior around the Rowers' Code with their partners. Tim felt a knot deep in his stomach.

Summary and Key Concepts

♦ For every point in the Rower's Code there are helping behaviors, those that help make you successful, and blocking behaviors, those that prevent success. Identifying your own personal strengths and weaknesses through this exercise will allow you to initiate positive change in your own behavior.

♦ Using a coach/partner to assess behavior can be helpful. Your partner can provide objective feedback on your self-observations. It also provides one-on-one time between teammates to further build their relationship.

Chapter 17

Fresh Air

When Tim and Christine walked out of the room to find a place to talk, Christine noticed that Tim's face was a bit flushed. "You don't look well. Are you okay?" she asked.

"Yes..." Tim hesitated, "Well...no. I'm not okay." He decided to take a chance and just get it out on the table. "This thing that happened with Doug has really affected me. I don't feel good about it at all."

Tim stood there shaking his head, feeling defeated, not knowing what to say. He couldn't believe he brought up the issue. But what else was he supposed to do? Months had gone by, and it felt as though the situation was getting out of hand. Every day he would go to work thinking it was the day he would get fired. Every night his wife would ask him if things were okay.

Tim's worry was getting in the way of his work. He used to be a risk-taker and it usually paid off. Now he was afraid to do anything. When Angela and Christine talked about being a bus rider, he thought to himself that he was turning into one, and that wasn't who he was. But he was afraid and he let it get in the way of being who he really was. Was it too late? He hoped it wasn't.

Opportunity to Talk

Christine could see by Tim's body language that he was very upset. "Tim, let's sit down and talk about it for a minute," she said gently. She began, "Before you say anything, I want you to know that I know what happened. I have been meaning to say something to you but haven't for a few reasons. One is that I wanted to get all the facts straight first; the other is that we just haven't had the opportunity to talk because I was out of the office last week and have been planning for this event. I know you have been doing a good job managing your department and your budget. I want you to rest assured that your job is not in jeopardy."

Not in jeopardy? Did I hear her right? Did she just say that my job is not in jeopardy? Tim lifted his head and looked at her. "You don't know how worried I have been. There have been so many rumors circulating. I moved all the way out here with my family from a town they loved out East. After what happened, I thought I had made a big mistake. I didn't know who to trust or what to do, really. I was paralyzed by it. Then you became my new boss. I have been afraid to approach you because I was fearful of what might happen."

"Well Tim, you don't have to be paralyzed by it any longer. As a matter of fact, I expect you to step up and do what we hired you for. Starting tomorrow, we are going to craft a strategy that will shape our future success, and I need you to carry your load and do your part. I'll do my best to set you up for success, and, as a team, we will do great things together. You can count on that."

Tim was shocked. All he could do was say thank you. After that, they had a great conversation during which they learned quite a lot more about each other. On the way back to the conference room, Tim sent his wife a text message telling her not to worry, that everything was fine at work.

Realization

Chip and Peter went outside and sat on the dock looking out at the water. Chip started talking first, of course. He explained that he didn't always consider the team in his decision-making. He excluded teammates he thought talked too much. Peter couldn't understand how Chip could say that, but he kept listening. After all, what choice did he have? Chip went on to say that his agenda was the only one he cared about. Peter listened.

As Chip was talking, he realized that his own behavior could end up excluding people and making them feel as though he didn't value their opinions or the work they did. Also, pushing his agenda so hard all the time wasn't always what was best for everyone else. The Rowers' Code was having a positive impact on him.

Chip continued by saying that, on a good note, he was straightforward in his communication and didn't talk outside of the boat. Peter listened intently as Chip talked.

When Chip was finally finished, he paused and looked at Peter, who took it as his queue to tell Chip a bit about himself. Peter told Chip how he had a hard time trusting his teammates, which often led to lack of commitment to the team. He didn't go directly to teammates when he had issues with them, but he didn't talk out of the boat either. He just kept things to himself.

Chip reminded him of what Angela said about doing nothing being just as bad as talking outside of the boat. Peter understood. He explained that his positive behavior was that he was good at timing and teeing up conversations. When he made appointments, he considered what worked best for the other person's schedule. He was very clear about why he wanted to meet, what they would discuss, and what he expected of them.

As a result of their meeting, Chip saw Peter in a new light, and he even took note of a few things he would try himself. Peter actually found it easy to talk to Chip. By the time they were ready to go back to the conference room, he realized that Chip had a lot to offer and that he should try to look past his personality and listen to what he had to say.

More Realization

It was easy for Marie and Nancy to talk to one another. Marie spoke about her issue of trying to do too much and over-committing. She was at a stage in her career at which she was in the process of building a strong network. To do that she joined several project groups and made sure she kept a busy social calendar. This sometimes led to not completing things as well as others expected, or not being as available as people needed her to be. She wasn't sure what to do about it, but she knew that she wanted to pay more attention to the quality of her work and her relationships. Nancy thought it was very mature of Marie to come to the realization that these factors were the keys to her success.

Nancy's positive behavior was that she sought out the opinions of others and considered them in her decision-making process. Also, she was great at doing her part and carrying her load. When she couldn't meet commitments, she told others well in advance so they could either find another resource to complete the work or adjust the schedule when it wasn't critical.

However, Nancy had a problem with timing, often speaking to people when it wasn't convenient for them. Nancy realized she needed to consider the bandwidth of others and what they had going on before trying to engage them in a conversation in the first place. Timing was important, especially when she expected others to make commitments and take action.

Honesty and Openness

The conversation between Dave and Doug was interesting. Dave was very honest when he told Doug he had problems realizing how his actions affected others on the team. He just didn't see how he could have so much influence. He saw himself as an individual contributor. He always trusted that if he kept on task and pushed ahead, he was doing his job.

On Friday afternoons, he would walk around the office doing status checks and collecting all kinds of information for a weekly status report to their boss. Some people on the team were extremely irritated by it. They even had given

Dave feedback that Friday afternoons were not the time to be doing that. They had also asked him to standardize the information he was requesting so they would know in advance what he wanted and could send it to him earlier in the week. That way, he could complete his report and get it to his boss by Friday at 5 p.m. Dave ignored them, and just kept asking for his various forms of information every Friday when it was convenient for him.

Now, he thought of Marie in the boat pushing Chip and wondered if his team felt that he was doing the same thing to them. Recently, when Chip needed his support, he withdrew it because Chip wouldn't give him what he wanted the Friday before. He knew it was childish, but he wanted to make a statement. It backfired. Chip made him look like a backstabbing idiot.

Doug didn't say much when it was his turn. He mumbled a few things about communication and talking outside the boat and then said, "Let's get some fresh air and go back to the room." Dave didn't argue, so Doug was happy.

Summary and Key Concepts

♦ We build trust through consistent application of values and behaviors. Begin with understanding another's situation, feelings, and motives, and encourage that person to learn from past mistakes. In this way, you will enhance the self-esteem of others and foster a team environment.

♦ Quite possibly the hardest art to master is understanding one's own knowledge, attitudes, and opinions as compared to others, as well as the way words and actions may impact team members. Being open to feedback and openly discussing one's own values and behaviors with others can improve both self-awareness and interactions.

Chapter 18

Two Boats and a Coach

When the team returned to the conference room, Angela sensed that something had changed. Chip had a thoughtful look on his face, Tim looked as though he had won the lottery, and Marie had calmed down. Christine looked content. The team was ready to engage.

When it was their turn to share with the whole team, Chip explained how he hadn't been giving every seat equal value and would need some help with listening skills. *Wow, I think he's getting it*, Tim thought.

Dave and Nancy each explained having a problem with timing. Marie and Tim felt off-balance, and Christine was trying to lead without taking over. Doug said he realized he needed to communicate better, but couldn't really explain what he meant by that or come up with an example.

Peter wanted to develop trust in his teammates, but while he was talking, Chip interrupted and said the reason they were doing this event was to build trust. Peter did not disagree. He explained that he was hoping the exercises they were doing that day would help them get to know one another better and develop trust. However, trust is built one interaction at a time. He knew it would take many interactions before he truly trusted anyone. The good news was that he was willing to give it a try. Many of them felt the same way—they just didn't say it.

Angela came to the conclusion that just as when they were in the boat, pairing off worked for them and they were able to communicate. However, when the whole team was in the room, they talked much less than when they paired off. To work through their issues and be successful as a team, they would have to also be able to communicate as a team. This hurdle was particularly difficult for them.

New Perspectives

The day's exercises had helped the team look at each other differently, and they were developing new perspectives of each other and the team. They had all made mistakes, but that was okay. Angela explained to them, "It's not the mistakes that matter so much; it's how you handle your mistakes and how you treat each other that counts."

"I have a question for you," she said. "What does *team* mean to you? As I said earlier, most people come from different corporate cultures. I would like to hear what you think of when you hear the word *team*."

Doug got out his iPhone and Googled "team." He spoke up. "Wikipedia says a team is a group of people or animals with a common purpose. A team of animals! Ha-ha!" *That's us*, he thought. "We have a common purpose, so we are a team."

Marie spoke up, "It's a group of people you work with. It's that simple."

"Is it?" Angela asked. "Are teams simple? I'm not so sure I agree with you. I think they can be simple, especially when you don't have major things you want to accomplish or when you don't expect much. But what about when you do? What about when you want to accomplish great things?"

"Then you rely on one another," said Chip.

"Rely on each other for what?" Angela asked.

The room became silent again. Everyone sat staring at Angela, waiting for her to continue. They all realized where this was going. They had never discussed what the word *team* meant or what their own team meant to them. If they wanted to be a winning team, first and foremost, they needed to agree on what it meant to them. Then their behavior needed to line up with their beliefs.

The Championship Boat

While Angela was getting ready to start the next exercise, she remembered an experience she recently had at the dock while waiting for boats to come in during practice. "I have a little story I'd like to tell you," she announced. "I was standing on the dock the other day waiting for the boats to come in after our morning crew team practice. The first team that came in was full of people who looked so enthusiastic. They were smiling and laughing—basically having a good time. I asked them what they were so happy about. They spoke right up and said that they had a great row and couldn't wait to rest up so they could come back to practice the next day.

"A few minutes later, a second team came in who didn't look as cheerful. They looked tired and had frustrated looks on their faces, so I asked them the same question. They answered saying that they couldn't wait to get off the dock and on with their day—mentioning nothing about coming back to row the next day. It was clear that rowing was already far from their minds.

"Their answer bothered me so I asked them how their row went. They said it went the way it always goes: just okay. Then, one by one, they started blaming each other for a bad row, making excuses and complaining. They said they felt tired and beat up from their hard practice that morning.

"I stood there thinking about the two conversations," Angela continued. "Both teams had said they rowed hard and were tired. While I was standing there, a person from the first team came back to the dock, and I asked her what they do when things don't go well. She said when things aren't going as expected, they stop the boat and figure out what each person could do to help. Then they focus on doing the right things right to help each other restore balance and get in sync.

"Someone from the second team also came back to the dock to pick up some equipment, so I asked him what his team does when the going gets tough. He said most of the time each member just does his or her own thing to compensate for a weakness and hope it all works out. He sounded very discouraged and very tired."

It was very clear to Angela and to most of the people in the room that, when the going got tough, the boat that did well and was motivated to return for another great day was the one in which everyone pulled together as a team. The boat that did poorly and was discouraged was the boat in which everyone did their own thing, pulling in different directions and not paying attention to each other. The scary thing was that their own team was much more like the second team, in which everyone pulled in their own direction when the going got tough.

Angela continued, "After all the teams finished rowing, I waited for the coaches to come back to the dock. When I saw the coach from the first team, I asked him what his biggest challenge was. He replied that he was responsible for 90 people. All 90 knew that there would be only one championship boat with nine people in it. So, his biggest challenge was making sure the other 81 people, who were not in the championship boat, had a sense of purpose and understood how important their role was to the success of the entire team. He lays out a clear vision and expectations, and they work towards them."

"If the other boats went out to practice every day without a sense of purpose and without knowing what was expected of them, the championship boat wouldn't have anyone to push them. They wouldn't be challenged. The coach said it is vitally important for each person, all 81 of them in the other boats, to understand how much their performance affected everyone else. He said that it's every leader's responsibility to help others understand their part in the dream. If they don't understand it, their individual performance decreases and the organization suffers."

She looked out at the group. They stared back.

"You are the championship boat," Angela said. "It's up to you to perform at your best and then go back to your own teams and help them understand how they are a part of the organization's success, how they are part of the dream. Without them and the work they do, the dream won't happen. You have to paint the vision for them, and then lead by example. You have to be the change you envision, because people don't follow a vision first; they follow a person."

Chip thought about what Angela said. This was a new way of looking at things, a new concept for him to consider. As a leader, Chip was used to communicating the vision and strategy, but it wasn't his style to get everyone to understand their part in it. He left that up to them.

Angela's words were powerful, and Chip reflected on them. If it was true that people follow a person first, and then a vision, then he wondered how people viewed him?. Chip had never questioned his leadership abilities before, but now he had a shadow of doubt about his performance.

Summary and Key Concepts

+ To be a championship team, you must recognize and use the skills of your team to continuously improve your performance. Provide training for team activities, facilitate a collaborative effort, remove obstacles, and recognize and reward success.

+ Throughout your organization you have people who contribute to the success of the company. Each individual, in some way, serves your customer, whether it is directly or through a process that leads to a customer service or product. Great performance requires individual excellence to achieve team goals.

Chapter 19

The 90 Percent Rule

Angela knew from experience as an elite rower that being able to picture success might help the team. Her coach would make them close their eyes and visualize what success would look like. Then they would put together a team success plan. They would identify their goals, strengths, weaknesses, and what to focus on.

Her coach had a special rule: they had to focus 90 percent of their effort on the things that made them successful and only 10 percent on their weaknesses. Her coach called it the 90 percent rule. The rule was important to make them continue building their strengths while they worked on their weaknesses.

"Do you know what your strengths are?" Angela challenged them. "Do you know the strengths of your teammates? Are you tapping into their strengths? Think about the positive behaviors we just discussed,

the things you said you were good at. These are the things you should make sure you keep doing. These are the things that made you successful so far."

Christine thought about what Angela had said and decided that she was right. Instead of focusing all their energy on the things they weren't doing right, they should make sure they put the majority of their effort into what was working for them. They needed to keep powering up their own boat with success.

Christine thought about management classes she had taken. Was she keeping up on her strengths? Maybe she should take some refresher courses. Times were changing rapidly, and the skills that had made her successful in the past would not necessarily be the ones that would carry her into the future.

Picture of Success

"I was lucky," Angela began. "I had a great coach. Every week he would post all of our accomplishments on a whiteboard in the boathouse. At the top of the board it said *Bean's Board of Success.* One day I asked him, 'Who is Bean? Some great rower?' He said, 'Nope. Bean stands for Patricia Beans, a woman I met on an airplane one day who told me about her success board at work, and I've used the idea ever since.'"

Christine loved the idea too, and could already picture it in their office. Each week they would have someone on the team collect their successes and post them on the team board. What a way to motivate the team!

"Is everyone ready to draw again?" Angela asked.

Doug wasn't. He was tired of the workshop and didn't see how it was going to help them. At this point he just wanted it to end so he could go and get his work done. He wished he could say so, but he was hoping that if he cooperated they would finish early and he could get out of there.

The rest of them were ready. They were eager to see how they could create their own boat like the one Angela described.

"I want you to draw a picture of the desired state of your team in boats again, like we did when you drew the current state," Angela continued. "Identify where you are rowing to and what you have to do to get there."

Christine was curious about what they would draw and didn't want to influence them, so she asked if it was okay for her to share her drawing last. They all agreed and started drawing.

They all drew essentially the same picture. The team was in one boat, the sun was shining, and they had smiles on their faces.

As they went around the room sharing their drawings, a common theme developed; of one boat rowing in the same direction towards opportunity, with Christine as their leader. The problem was that no one identified what the opportunity was or any of the issues they would have to row through. The water they were rowing through was calm. There were no other boats in the water either—no danger, no competition. It looked very unrealistic.

Summary and Key Concepts

♦ Success begins with a clear and compelling picture of the desired future state. Organizations are made up of complex areas with many individuals. To facilitate alignment of people and other resources, a detailed vision is required. Vision provides a positive view of the future and should be created by the team so that everyone feels passionate about it and can inspire others to follow it.

♦ Core competencies help an organization to succeed by identifying its unique strength and leveraging it to many markets and products. Understand your own strengths so that you can leverage them for the benefit of the team.

Chapter 20

Rock the Boat

When the team members finished sharing their drawings, Angela wrote "Rock the Boat" on the whiteboard. She was convinced they were afraid of dealing with their issues.

"What is 'rock the boat'?" asked Marie.

"Rocking the boat is a way to bring up issues and challenges without damaging your relationships," Angela explained. "The overall purpose of it is to gain understanding and avoid misunderstanding, so that you can address issues and make decisions that are fact-based.

"You rock the boat to gain balance and alignment. I know it might sound funny to you, and I'm sure that at times people have told you *not* to rock the boat, but you can't have a stable, solid boat without rocking it and seeing what it's made of."

They all knew exactly what she meant. She was right, but they were all afraid because they didn't know how to rock the boat without hurting each other and their relationships.

Angela continued, "You experienced rocking the boat out on the water. Remember the drill that had you raise and lower your hands? Even as more people rowed and things got more complicated, the boat rocked, but you didn't tip it over. Instead, as it got more complicated, you listened to Kim and Bill's feedback, and the feedback of your peers, and worked it out together."

Angela continued. "You stabilize the boat together. It wasn't that simple though. At one point you had to step back a bit and slow down. If you didn't get any feedback, it could have been disastrous, especially when a few of you let go of your oars."

"I'd like you to start rocking the boat during the rest of the work we will do today and then continue doing it tomorrow and in the future."

Angela wrote some guidelines on the whiteboard under the title "Rock the Boat Ground Rules":

- Use the Rowers' Code as your guide.
- Focus on the issue or challenge at hand.
- Separate facts from opinions.
- Seek first to understand and second to be understood.
- Show interest. Listen while others are talk-ing. If you are spending your time and energy

framing up how you want to say something, you can't hear what others are saying

♦ Divide what has been said into two categories: the points you agree on and the points you disagree on.

♦ Ask open-ended and clarifying questions: What observations have you made? Why do you feel the way you do? Is there additional supporting data or facts that would be helpful?

♦ No personal attacks.

♦ No zaps.

♦ When emotions start running too high, take a break.

"What's a zap?" Marie asked.

"Zaps are discouraging comments such as 'that's stupid,' 'we can't do that,' 'it won't work,' or 'we've already tried that." You also shouldn't sigh, roll your eyes, or show other aggressive or passive-aggressive behavior," answered Angela.

Peter saw Marie get out her phone. "What are you doing?" asked Peter.

"I'm looking up passive-aggressive behavior on Wikipedia."

"What does it say?"

Everyone wanted to hear the definition. Marie read it out loud: "Passive-aggressive behavior refers to passive, sometimes obstructionist resistance to following through with expectations in interpersonal or occupational situations. It can manifest itself as learned help lessness, procrastination, stubbornness, resentment, sullenness, or deliberate/repeated failure to accomplish requested tasks for which one is (often explicitly) responsible. It is a defense mechanism, and (more often than not) only partly conscious. For example, suppose someone does not wish to attend a party. A passive-aggressive response in that situation might involve taking so long to get ready that the party is nearly over by the time they arrive."

Doug was embarrassed. Was wearing a suit considered passive-aggressive? Probably, he thought. After all, he *did* do it to get out of rowing.

Examining Behaviors

Angela passed out a summary sheet of the Rowers' Code. Using it and the Rock the Boat Ground Rules, the team spent the next hour brainstorming behaviors that could help them be successful and behaviors that could hinder them.

The Rowers' Code Summary Sheet

#1 Always Do What's Best for the Team.	Putting the interests of your team in front of your own. Rowing as "one boat" instead of everyone rowing in his or her own direction.	Commitment
#2 Give Every Seat Equal Value.	Treating others with respect. Acknowledging and trusting in each other's strengths.	Acknowledgement
#3 Carry Your Load.	Knowing and doing your share of what needs to be done.	Responsibility
#4 Balance the Boat.	Attaining the right mix of people and skills on your team to meet your goals.	Organizational and self-awareness
#5 Stay in Sync.	Timing is everything. Realizing that everything you do affects others. Knowing your bandwidth and the bandwidth of others.	Situational awareness
#6 Lead by Example.	Trusting in yourself and others. Sharing leadership responsibility.	Trust
#7 Keep Everything in the Boat.	Communicating clearly and honestly with your teammates.	Integrity

Although they were tired, almost everyone pitched in, and they came up with several positive behaviors they should do and several negative behaviors they wanted to stop doing. A few zaps flew around the room and a few times passive-aggressive behavior emerged, but it was nothing like any of their previous meetings. During the exercise, the team started to feel some positive energy. It was refreshing.

Here's what they came up with:

#1 Always Do What's Best for the Team		
Things to do		**Things to stop doing**
1. Consider the impact your actions have on the team.		1. Acting like you agree on something you don't.
2. Take responsibility for team decisions.		2. Making decisions in a vacuum.
3. Keep stakeholders well informed.		3. Throwing team members under the bus.
4. Align resources with priorities.		4. Being selfish with resources.
5. Show support through action.		5. Making discouraging remarks.
6. Pitch in when others need help or resources.		6. Exhibiting passive-aggressive behavior.
7. Put the team first.		

#2 Give Every Seat Equal Value		
Things to do		**Things to stop doing**
1. Listen and take interest when others talk, present, and need input. 2. Include everyone's input in team decisions. 3. Switch roles to understand each other's responsibility and challenges. 4. Hear people out. Let them complete what they have to say.		1. Talking over others, interrupting, allowing others to interrupt. 2. Asking for advice, but not acting on it. 3. Showing favoritism. 4. Not taking others seriously.

#3 Carry Your Load		
Things to do		**Things to stop doing**
1. Honor your promises/ commitments. 2. Understand expectations. 3. Share work evenly. 4. If you can't meet an obligation, find a way/resource yourself to get it done. 5. Turn work in on time, meeting expectations.		1. Piling work on others. 2. Having unrealistic expectations. 3. Making promises you know you can't keep. 4. Submitting work that's not up to par. 5. Blaming others. 6. Complaining about workload after the fact. 7. Turning work in late.

#4 Balance the Boat		
Things to do		**Things to stop doing**
1. Put the right people in the right roles.		1. Allowing overbearing behavior.
2. Gather input from everyone.		2. Making one-sided decisions.
3. Include everyone in team decisions.		3. Distributing uneven workloads.
4. Distribute responsibility evenly.		4. Having double standards.
5. Give equal opportunity to everyone.		5. Putting people in the wrong roles.
6. Understand what people can and cannot do.		6. Having unfilled positions.
		7. Having unrealistic expectations.

#5 Stay in Sync		
Things to do		**Things to stop doing**
1. Communicate clearly. 2. Ensure the team is on board with decisions and action plans before moving forward. 3. Hold regular status updates. 4. Show empathy. 5. Understand the bandwidth of your peers. 6. Be more accommodating.		1. Miscommunicating. 2. Barging in while others are in the middle of something. 3. Moving forward when everyone isn't on board. 4. Being demanding and forcing issues. 5. Assuming anything.

#6 Lead by Example		
Things to do		**Things to stop doing**
1. Hold yourself to the same standard to which you hold everyone else. 2. Listen to everyone equally. 3. Be proactive on high-priority issues.		1. Interrupting. 2. Forcing your opinion. 3. Acting like you are in the know. 4. Arriving late, leaving early. 5. Thinking rules don't apply to you the same way they do to others.

#7 Keep Everything in the Boat		
Things to do		**Things to stop doing**
1. Directly communicate with teammates when you have an issue. 2. Bring things out in the open. 3. Encourage open and honest communication. 4. Seek to understand while listening. 5. Be part of the solution.		1. Airing dirty laundry with others outside the team. 2. Pushing things under the rug. 3. Not telling others how you really feel. 4. Gossiping. 5. Complaining inside and outside the team without offering solutions.

Angela asked team members to pair up with the same partners they had in the earlier exercises. They would now be accountability partners. They were to set dates to meet the following week, so they could assess their progress. She told them she would send out an e-mail with some information to help them stay focused on positive behavior and track their progress with their accountability partners.

Doug thought the whole exercise was ridiculous. He went through the motions, as he had many times before, with no intention of following through.

Looking Forward to Change

Most of the others were looking forward to seeing the impact of their effort. They were starting to become a real team. They were even looking forward to the start of their strategic planning session the next day, something they normally dreaded. A relaxing dinner that night would help get them ready for the work in front of them.

Summary and Key Concepts

♦ A strong and growing team will bring up difficult issues and challenges in order to gain understanding, allowing those issues to be addressed in a fact-based manner. "Rocking the boat" will allow you to gain balance and alignment, and help you to come to a conclusion and move forward as a team.

♦ When discussing issues, follow the Rowers' Code while being respectful of other people's opinions. Address issues in a forthright manner, avoiding passive-aggressive behavior and discouraging comments.

Chapter 21

Wrap Up

It was time to wrap things up. Angela asked if anyone had anything they wanted to bring up before they closed for the day. Christine answered with, "Yes, I would. I'd like to bring up Chip's drawing." Chip's face turned red. He thought they had moved on. His stomach sank. Christine continued. "In Chip's drawing there were some empty seats."

"I didn't mean..." interrupted Chip.

"Chip, just wait, let me finish," she said, smiling. "Chip said he thought we had the wrong mix. I agree with him but not in the same way. We have the right mix of people, but the wrong mix of what to focus on. When I reviewed the previous strategic plan, I saw way too many items on it. The answer isn't necessarily to reset the people in the boat; it's to reset the plan.

"As a team, you couldn't possibly have had the bandwidth to deal with everything you had in it. It assumed everything would go perfectly well. But, as we all know from our experience today, in the blink of an eye, things can change, just like the water and the weather did. When it does, we need to be able to pull together. Before our meeting tomorrow, I want you to ask yourself a few questions:

1. Do we want to do many things in a mediocre way or do we want to do a few things really well?

2. What are our real issues?

3. What are our opportunities?

"I believe our team has huge potential," Christine continued. "But, we will have to focus as a team to be successful in the challenging environment we live in. Things are changing rapidly, just like when we were in the boat today and everything changed so quickly. When that happened, Kim asked us to lead by example and focus on the back of the person in front of us. I want you to also consider leading by example and watching the backs of your teammates as we construct our new strategy. For some of you, it will mean shifts in budget, people, time, and energy. It won't be easy. But, if we work together like the way we did today we will be successful and accomplish things we never thought we could.

"If you are worried about some items being taken out the strategy, it doesn't mean they can't be put back in later. Let's consider what's best for the whole team first. As some items get checked off we can add others back in."

In general, they all agreed with what she was saying; they just didn't know how it would affect them or what process they would use to build the new strategy. Christine could see concern on their faces, and continued.

"We didn't really have a chance to practice rocking the boat much today, but, as we identify our issues and challenges, we can start doing that. We will definitely use the method when we start working on the new strategy tomorrow and as part of the way we work together in the future.

"I expect all of you to bring your issues and opportunities to the table tomorrow. As a matter of fact, I've asked Angela to stick with us and help coach us through them. She will also help coach us around our Rowers' Code behaviors so we have the best boat for moving forward."

Everyone felt relieved. Angela was a great facilitator and had already moved them through quite a lot of rough water.

Christine announced that they would have an hour break before dinner.

Recall

During the break Christine called home, quickly checked her e-mail, and went for a walk to relax and think through her dinner speech. During her walk, she recalled what individuals said during the exercise in which they talked about behaviors that were helping them and those that weren't.

The team identified several behaviors they needed to start doing and several behaviors they needed to stop. How would they change? How would they make it happen? While she was thinking about it, she realized there were a few people to whom she would need to give special attention. She remembered a conversation she had a few months back with a ship employee, Carmen, she met on a cruise in Hawaii.

Carmen had several buttons on her jacket, and one day Christine asked her what they were for. Carmen answered that most of them were standard buttons that everyone had on the ship, pointing to each one and explaining what it was. She missed one button, a small gold star, so Christine asked about that one. Carmen blushed and said it was for being a good employee.

Christine then asked her what her biggest challenges were with her team. Carmen told her that employees come with different work experiences, so she tries to learn the most about their background. Once she does, she uses her knowledge to help guide her staff. Additionally, Carmen makes sure her staff knows she cares about them. Every week she holds a meeting to listen to what they have to say and to share ideas.

Christine was very impressed with Carmen. It was clear that Carmen was dedicated to her team and very proud of them too. She liked what Carmen said about people needing to know you care. In the past, Christine had expected new people on her team to be team players and to hit the ground running. A few times she was disappointed by an individual's performance and couldn't understand why he kept talking about how he did things on his old team. Now she realized she needed to consider her employees' previous work experiences in her expectations.

Christine thought of what her friend Jane said about Notre Dame football coach Lou Holtz, known for his quick wit and ability to inspire others. According to Jane, Holtz used to say that there were three things a team needs to know from their coach:

1. That he or she wants to do a good job.

2. That they can trust him or her.

3. That he or she cares about them.

Christine asked herself if she met the three criteria. The first one was a given; of course everyone knew she wanted to do a good job. The second point would take time, because she was new to the team and trust isn't developed overnight. As for the third point, Christine cared about each one of her team members, but she wasn't quite sure they knew it. It was something she would have to work on. Using the Rowers' Code would be a good start.

Summary and Key Concepts

♦   Each team member looks up to his or her leader for encouragement and guidance. It is not enough to have a good plan. The leader must show that he or she cares for the team and trust that its members will give their all.

Chapter 22

The Dinner

At dinner, Christine started by thanking everyone for coming to the offsite and for working hard that day. In the moments leading up to her speech, she realized how important it was for the team to understand that it wasn't up to her to "save" them, as Chip had implied in his drawing.

"Looking at our competitive landscape and industry challenges, I need everyone to understand that we are in a boat, just like the boat we rowed in today. I need each person to get in, own their seat, and row. We have serious challenges ahead of us, which will require you to row together for long periods of time. To power up our boat, each person has to understand where we are going and what they can personally do to help us get there."

"We can't row our boat until it's balanced and aligned. I know our boat hasn't always been aligned or balanced—sometimes it has gone in the wrong direction—but today is a new day. Today is the day we started learning about how to really work together and how to become aligned with one another. We brainstormed the positive behaviors we want to support, as well as the behaviors we will not tolerate, because they are not helping us."

Commitment and Value

Christine continued, "This is a serious commitment. I am expecting all of us to work together to do what's best for the team by putting the team in front of ourselves. To do that, we have to trust each other and know that we will back each other through thick and thin, good times and bad. We need to understand the demands of each seat on the team, respect the challenges of each role, and give equal value to every person on the team.

"From our rowing experience today, I learned we should never underestimate the value of each person's contribution to success and never take for granted what it requires for each person to carry his or her load and maintain balance on our team. Moving forward, I expect each one of you to work on improving your strengths and acknowledging your weaknesses, so we can work as a team to overcome any obstacle. I expect everyone to keep our issues in our own boat, where we will work them out openly and honestly.

"I learned so much about each of you today, and I am proud of all of you. It wasn't easy trying a sport that takes so much coordination and team effort, but you did it—we did it. I want us to commit to doing excellent work together

every day. I want you to know you can trust me and that I care about each and every one of you. Every person on this team is important to me, and we are important to our company. Together we will make our company successful. I believe in us."

Critical Moment

Then Christine said something totally unexpected. "I also have an apology. I left the room today during a critical moment, when were setting the boat. I have to say, I was proud of all of you, because you quickly stepped up when I stepped out. But, I also want you to know that I am not perfect. I am human and I also make mistakes. Angela said today that it's not that we make mistakes; mistakes happen. It's how we handle them that matters most.

"I can assure you, there will be rough waters ahead. But, I can also assure you that by sticking together, we will overcome these hard times. We can do all these things I am talking about by embracing the Rowers' Code and dedicating ourselves to keeping it."

"The energy in the room this afternoon and evening is so positive and refreshing. This is a great start to our meeting and to our new strategic plan. Thank you, Angela, for all that you've done for us today."

With that, the team clapped and cheered. They all agreed with Christine and looked as though they were looking forward to working on their new plan—except Doug, who seemed as if he wasn't even paying attention.

Summary and Key Concepts

+ Never underestimate the value of each person's contribution to success, and never take for granted what it takes for each person to carry his or her load and maintain balance on your team.

+ Michael Jordan, one of history's greatest basketball players and athletes, is quoted as saying, "Talent wins games, but teamwork and intelligence win championships." To power up your boat, each person on the team has to understand where you all are going and what he or she can personally do to help get you there.

Chapter 23

Timing Is Everything

After dinner, while Christine was on her way back to her room, she got a text message and sat down in the lobby to answer it. As Christine was typing, she overheard Doug telling Peter that he thought it was a wasted day. She wished she had never sat down and had just kept walking.

Doug and Peter just happened to be right around the corner from where she sat. They couldn't see her and she couldn't see them, but she could certainly hear their voices—loud and clear. There was no mistaking them. Her heart sank as she listened to their conversation.

"These things don't matter," Doug said. "They are all the same. In a few days we won't even remember it."

Peter responded, "That's not true, Doug. It does matter. I know I'll remember it."

"Well aren't you special," replied Doug. "You have no idea what it's like to be on this team. Let me tell you, you're the only one who..."

Peter cut him off. "You're right, I am just getting to know this team. But, I'm not the only one who got something out of today. Many of us did. It was great."

"Well, it wasn't great for me. I ruined my favorite suit," Doug exclaimed. He was still angry at himself for wearing it.

"I guess you should have come prepared."

"Look, Peter, I'm just trying to help you. I don't mean anything bad by it, I just don't want you to be let down when you see how things really work and how everyone really is, not all this mumbo jumbo, kumbaya stuff."

"I don't know, Doug. I saw how everyone really is today, and I like what I saw. I want to give it a try. I believe in what we did. This was different. All the other teambuilding things I've ever done weren't like this. I'm proud of what we did together. We made mistakes, but we also made progress. I learned some lessons I'll never forget. Anyway, let's drop the subject; there's no talking outside the boat."

"I'm talking to you and you're in my boat."

"Come on Doug, you know what I mean. If you had all these problems, why didn't you bring them up today? We agreed to work on issues as a team. Listen, I'm tired, and I need to get some sleep. Good night."

Peter didn't wait for Doug to say one more word, he just turned and walked away while Doug stood there staring at him.

Taking Action

Christine wanted to crawl under a rock. *He has got to go*, she thought. *How could he act like that after everything we did today?* Peter was right. Doug had every chance to speak up and he didn't. She waited a few minutes before getting up to go back to her room so Doug could walk away without knowing she heard them.

On the way back she decided to stop and get a bottle of water. As she was walking out of the store, she almost ran smack into Doug.

"Hi, Doug."

"Hi, Christine. How's it going?"

"Pretty good. I'm a bit tired. It was a long day today. How about you? Are you enjoying our offsite?"

"It's great," Doug replied.

"Really?" she asked.

Christine couldn't believe her ears. *Was this the same guy that was trashing everyone and everything a few minutes before? How can he lie like this? Why can't he tell the truth?*

"Yes, I think we are on the right track," he continued. "I got so much out of it today."

Christine asked herself, *Do I deal with this now, or deal with it later?* She was tired from a long day of activities. She just wanted to go back to her room, crawl into bed, and get some sleep. As she reached into her pocket for her room key, she felt something else in her pocket. It was the tiny rubber chicken Angela gave her earlier that day to remind her to *not* be a chicken. She weighed the situation quickly in her head and said, "Doug, I think you and I should talk."

Summary and Key Concepts

- Openness, honesty, and decisive action are essential to team success with the Rowers' Code. It's preferable to cut off bad behavior at the pass rather than clean up after it at a later time. The amount of time and energy saved is well worth the effort up front.

- A pivotal point in any team member's life is the choice to stay both physically and mentally on a team. The most destructive employees are those who choose to stay on a team but have checked out on every other dimension of performance. It is the leader's responsibility to assure each team member is 100 percent present and rowing for the good of the team.

Chapter 24

Sweet Dreams

Chip was exhausted by the time his head hit the pillow. He fell into a deep sleep almost immediately. Suddenly, he was sitting in a chair in his office staring down at his hand. In his hand was the tiny, yellow rubber chicken Angela gave him. It started moving, and then it stood up and was looking right at him. His eyes opened wide.

The chicken spoke. "Chip, I have something I would like to tell you."

Chip shook his head. "What?" You can't talk!" he exclaimed.

"Sure I can! Now, listen to me," the chicken replied, peering at him.

Chip couldn't believe his eyes. His chicken was talking to him! He took a breath, blinked his eyes, and waited to see if it would go away. It didn't. It was still standing up in his hand and it had one wing in the air as though it was going to declare something.

"Now, listen to me Chip. You have a bright future in front of you. But you are missing something," the chicken said.

"What? What am I missing?" he asked.

"Leadership skills," the chicken said.

"That's ridiculous; I was born a leader."

The chicken smiled at him and continued. "Sure, you often command attention and take control. But, every great leader knows they need other people to really make a difference in the world. You act like you don't need anybody. "

"Now wait a minute," Chip replied. "I never said I didn't need anyone."

"Well, action speaks louder than words," the chicken replied. "In reality, Chip, you have not reached one tenth of your potential."

"Really?" Chip questioned.

"Really," the chicken replied nodding its head in confidence. "And I'll tell you why. Because you try doing things yourself all the time, when you really need help or when you have to make a difficult decision, you don't reach out to your team. You've developed a habit of thinking that you have all the information you need and there is really nothing else to consider. You limit your resources and don't capitalize on the strengths of your team. In fact Chip, you aren't really leading at all.

"To make it worse, you're so used to doing it, that you don't even think other people notice. But they do, Chip. People don't follow words, people follow people."

"I know, I know—people follow people" Chip replied in frustration.

"Yes, it's true. Your behavior excludes others, then they become hesitant to work with you, and at times some even resent you as their leader. You sense it sometimes and interact with them even less. It's a vicious cycle. I'd like to help you break it."

The chicken was now lying in his hand on it's back with it's wings behind its head and it's feet crossed. All it needed was a hammock.

"Okay, what do I do?"

"You can start by giving every seat equal value and leading by example. If you want people to value you, you have to value them first. You must realize that everyone's role, experiences, and talent are valuable. Everyone has something to offer, something that can help you and the team succeed," the chicken responded, standing up pointing one wing in the air and pacing like a college professor.

"Okay, go on." Chip was now listening eagerly.

"Start with behavior that shows you believe in your peers. Ask them questions, get their input, and act on what they say. If they're talking to you, don't cut them off, talk over them, or tune them out"

Chip knew the chicken was right. In fact, this conversation was already longer than most of the ones he had with his own team. He didn't take the time to actually discuss things with his team; he usually just moved forward with his own agenda. He had stopped asking people for their opinions, because he thought it would take too long to hear them out, and, even worse, he may have to act on what they said, rather than do what he wanted.

The chicken went on. "Furthermore, when you do ask people questions, you don't even wait for them to answer. Why do you bother asking?"

"To be honest, I think they hold me back," Chip answered. But it wasn't true. He worked with talented people, but he never took the time to find out what their strengths were, fearing they would challenge him.

"Hold you back?" the chicken said with its beak wide open. "The only thing holding you back is yourself. Change your behavior so that it becomes an example for others. If you want others to value your opinion and strengths, you have to value theirs. If you want to do great things, Chip, you need a team. You can't be a great leader without a team to lead." Chip was staring at the chicken when it suddenly disappeared.

He awoke, and his tiny chicken was laying on the night-stand next to his bed. "You're not going to try talking to me are you?" The chicken didn't answer him. It didn't even move.

Breakfast Discussion

When Chip arrived at the dining room, almost every-one was already sitting down having breakfast.

"How did you sleep?" Tim asked.

"I had the weirdest dream," Chip replied. "The rubber chicken Angela gave us came to life and was talking to me."

"That *is* weird," Tim responded, laughing. "What did the chicken say?"

"Oh, the chicken said a lot of things. The funny part is it was all true."

"Well that's good," Tim said. "There's nothing worse than a yellow rubber chicken that comes to life and lies to you." They both laughed.

◆◆◆

Marie noticed that Doug was not in the room. *Maybe he stayed at the bar a bit too late last night*, she thought.

Peter sat down next to her.

"Good morning," he said with a smile on his face.

"Good morning," Marie replied, smiling back at him.

Peter hadn't been on the team very long, but Marie liked how he conducted himself and what he had to say. He seemed genuinely interested in what others had to say as well.

"What did you think about the Rock the Boat exercise?" she asked.

"It was different for me." Peter responded. "I'm not used to people being so forward in bringing up issues and challenges. On the teams I've been on in the past, it wasn't okay to bring things up that way."

Marie kept listening.

"I like what we did. I hope we can continue to use that exercise. It felt good to be able to discuss our behavior and set a new bar for how we want to work together."

"I liked it too," said Marie. "Getting things done is really important to me. Sometimes I feel that people waste so much energy avoiding the problem. If we could use Rock the

Boat to focus on the real issues and gaining understanding to make solid business decisions, it would certainly save a lot of time and energy."

"Yeah. Just hearing each other out yesterday seemed to have a big impact. I thought it was funny how we all basically agreed on some things we thought we disagreed on earlier."

"Yeah, that was weird," Marie replied. "Talking about things certainly clears up assumptions and misunderstandings."

◆◆◆

Chip, Dave, and Christine all ate breakfast in silence. Each of them was deep in thought about the work they were about to do that day.

After the chicken dream, Chip made a goal of listening to his peers and being supportive. He didn't want to dominate conversations as he had done in the past. The exercises the day before made it clear to him that he wasn't bringing as much value to the table as he thought by being the first one to speak up all the time. His peers were smart, and they had good things to say. He just needed to listen to them.

Dave was trying to think of a way he could bring up the Friday reporting without everyone tossing him out of the boat. What he didn't realize is that they didn't want to toss him out. He was good at what he did; it was his process that irritated them. As he ate, he ran scenarios through his head about how to bring it up without causing mutiny.

Christine was deep in thought about her conversation with Doug. It was time to get started.

Summary and Key Concepts

♦ Examine your professional behavior to assess whether you are doing what's right for your team. Your teammates expect as much from you as you expect from them.

Chapter 25

Clearing the Deck

Everyone was present, except Doug. When Christine stood up to talk, Chip asked, "Has anyone seen Doug? I called his room, but he didn't answer." All heads turned to Christine.

She responded quickly, "I was just about to tell you Doug won't be joining us. He has decided to leave the team."

"What?" asked Chip. "Are you joking?"

"It's not a joke," explained Christine. "Doug and I had a talk last night, and he feels this is not the right team for him." The room fell silent. Christine was prepared for the worst. She wasn't sure how the team would react. He had worked with them for several years. She waited for more comments, but the room remained silent. She stood there looking at them and realized that maybe they were glad he was gone.

They heard a knock on the door, and it opened. It was Doug. "Excuse me," he said, looking sheepish.

"Yes, Doug, come in. We were just talking about your news," Christine said.

Doug took a step into the room and the door closed behind him. "I just wanted to apologize to everyone, especially you, Christine," he said looking directly at her. "I couldn't sleep last night after our talk. I sat up thinking about all the changes we have gone through as a team the last several months and how they've been difficult for all of us. My conduct hasn't always made things easier, so I'm sorry for my behavior during the last few months, and especially during the past few days."

Everyone was astonished.

Doug continued, "Last night I realized that though I have had opportunities to step up and lead by example, I instead acted poorly and have not been a good team member."

They all stared at him in disbelief. Marie and several others wondered what Christine could have said to him the night before. What could have compelled Doug to first leave the team and then to apologize?

Doug continued, "Furthermore, I'd like to stay on the team if it's still possible."

He paused, waiting for Christine to respond. She didn't.

"If it's not possible, I completely understand," he mumbled, looking down at his shoes, waiting for Christine to answer.

"Well," Christine replied, "I'm glad you thought about what we discussed. And, actually, I'm glad you changed your mind." Turning to the team, she said, "Why don't we take a break while Doug and I chat for a few minutes, and then we'll get started with our agenda for the day. We'll start again in 15 minutes."

With that, Christine turned to Doug and said, "Let's go find a place to chat for a few minutes." He nodded and followed her out the door to look for a private place to talk.

Heart to Heart

Doug and Christine found a spot far enough away from the team where no one could overhear them.

"So Doug, what made you change your mind?" she asked.

"It was the chicken," he replied, feeling silly.

"The chicken?" she asked. "Why the chicken?"

He felt foolish. "Well, last night while changing out of my clothes, the chicken fell out of my pocket. When I picked it up off the floor and looked at it, I thought, *Who's the real chicken?* All this time, I could have been honest and told you and the team what I thought. I could have contributed to our discussions instead of being like a stick in your wheel. When things got difficult or when I didn't know what to do, I chickened out. I decided that what I need to do most is to change my own behavior and become a contributor again, an asset instead of a liability."

"Wow, that's something," Christine said. "Well, we sure could use all your years of experience," Christine stated. "But are you going to stick by this team through good and bad times, and keep everything in the boat when things don't go the way you think they should?"

"Well, it will take some practice, and I'll need to work closely with my accountability partner, but I *think* I can do it," he said.

"I need to know you *will* do it," she answered, looking right at him. "You see," she said, "this is where commitment comes in. I need to know that you are part of this team. The decisions we make throughout the next few days and weeks ahead will be *our* decisions, not mine. I need each member of the team to own them just as much as I do. Can I count on you Doug?" she asked.

"Yes," he said, knowing this time he wanted to commit to the team. "You can count on me."

Summary and Key Concepts

- Mistakes happen. What counts is how you handle them.

- Commitment creates a winning team. Without committing one's best in every aspect of the Rowers' Code, the team will not succeed.

- The Rowers' Code applies well beyond the confines of a boat. The work team that lives by these elements of working together, and supporting and respecting each person and his or her role, will achieve what no individual could achieve alone.

Chapter 26

Next Strokes

When everyone returned to the room, Christine began the strategic planning session by sharing the environmental assessment, which included the competitive landscape, customer needs, industry changes, and internal core competencies.

And that wasn't all they did. Armed with the right information, they developed a plan to close the gap between their current state and their vision for the future.

During the next few months, Doug wasn't the only one who made great strides. Chip learned to value his peers and put his trust in them, which produced great returns. Dave started considering the bandwidth of others, standardized report templates, and stopped making unreasonable demands.

Marie asked Nancy to be her mentor, and Nancy happily accepted. Tim was working hard on his IT deliverables, meeting tough timelines he set for himself. Peter developed the trust he needed to commit to the team and it paid off big. Christine loved working with the team and was very proud of them. Finally, they were rowing as a team.

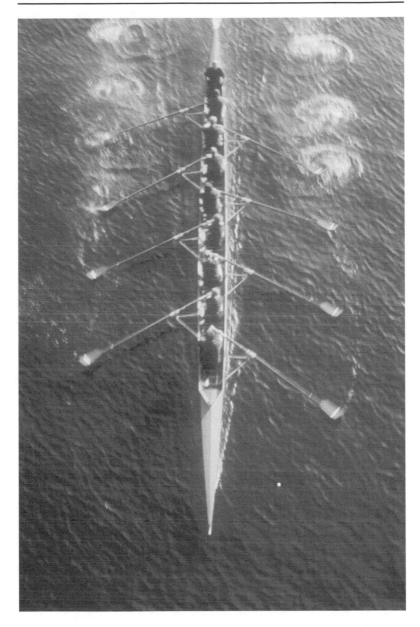

Appendix A

Team Assessment

The team assessment on the following pages is designed to help you evaluate the current state of your team. You can complete the questionnaire in this book or online as a team on our Website at *www.rowerscode.com*, where we will tabulate the results and send you a report.

Circle the response to the following statements that most closely matches how you feel about your team's behavior. Only circle one response per statement. When you have completed the questionnaire, combine the scores for each page and summarize them for a grand total using the table at the end of the questionnaire.

1. We put the interests of the team in front of our personal goals and ambitions.

    a. strongly agree
    b. agree
    c. slightly agree
    d. slightly disagree
    e. disagree
    f. strongly disagree

2. We consistently behave in ways that show our commitment to the team.

    a. strongly agree
    b. agree
    c. slightly agree
    d. slightly disagree
    e. disagree
    f. strongly disagree

3. When a decision is made, we show support by our proactive actions.

    a. strongly agree
    b. agree
    c. slightly agree
    d. slightly disagree
    e. disagree
    f. strongly disagree

Number of responses for statements 1–3:

a.___ b.___ c.___ d.___ e.___ f.___

4. We have the right mix of people on our team to reach our goals.

   a. strongly agree

   b. agree

   c. slightly agree

   d. slightly disagree

   e. disagree

   f. strongly disagree

5. As a team, we maximize each other's strengths and minimize each other's weaknesses.

   a. strongly agree

   b. agree

   c. slightly agree

   d. slightly disagree

   e. disagree

   f. strongly disagree

6. We understand the importance of how individual performance leads to team success.

   a. strongly agree

   b. agree

   c. slightly agree

   d. slightly disagree

   e. disagree

   f. strongly disagree

Number of responses for statements 4–6:

a.___ b.___ c.___ d.___ e.___ f.___

7. We hold ourselves and each other accountable.
    a. strongly agree
    b. agree
    c. slightly agree
    d. slightly disagree
    e. disagree
    f. strongly disagree

8. Team performance is discussed openly and honestly.
    a. strongly agree
    b. agree
    c. slightly agree
    d. slightly disagree
    e. disagree
    f. strongly disagree

9. We inform each other well in advance if we cannot keep a commitment or perform as expected.
    a. strongly agree
    b. agree
    c. slightly agree
    d. slightly disagree
    e. disagree
    f. strongly disagree

Number of responses for statements 7–9:

a.___ b.___ c.___ d.___ e.___ f.___

10. We have a clear understanding of the goals of the team.

    a. strongly agree

    b. agree

    c. slightly agree

    d. slightly disagree

    e. disagree

    f. strongly disagree

11. We have reasonable and achievable goals.

    a. strongly agree

    b. agree

    c. slightly agree

    d. slightly disagree

    e. disagree

    f. strongly disagree

12. We understand what we are personally expected to do to reach the goals of the team.

    a. strongly agree

    b. agree

    c. slightly agree

    d. slightly disagree

    e. disagree

    f. strongly disagree

Number of responses for statements 10–12:

a.___ b.___ c.___ d.___ e.___ f.___

13. We are good at prioritizing what we need to focus on as individuals.

    a. strongly agree

    b. agree

    c. slightly agree

    d. slightly disagree

    e. disagree

    f. strongly disagree

14. We help each other out, sometimes dropping what we are doing or reassigning resources.

    a. strongly agree

    b. agree

    c. slightly agree

    d. slightly disagree

    e. disagree

    f. strongly disagree

15. We are masters of great timing, considering each other and how our actions affect them.

    a. strongly agree

    b. agree

    c. slightly agree

    d. slightly disagree

    e. disagree

    f. strongly disagree

Number of responses for statements 13–15:

a.___ b.___ c.___ d.___ e.___ f.___

16. Our leaders value our perspective and seek it out.

   a. strongly agree

   b. agree

   c. slightly agree

   d. slightly disagree

   e. disagree

   f. strongly disagree

17. Everyone on the team plays an active role in decision-making.

   a. strongly agree

   b. agree

   c. slightly agree

   d. slightly disagree

   e. disagree

   f. strongly disagree

18. We feel there is a commitment to integrity and ethical practices.

   a. strongly agree

   b. agree

   c. slightly agree

   d. slightly disagree

   e. disagree

   f. strongly disagree

Number of responses for statements 16–18:

a.___ b.___ c.___ d.___ e.___ f.___

19. We communicate openly and honestly with each other.

    a. strongly agree

    b. agree

    c. slightly agree

    d. slightly disagree

    e. disagree

    f. strongly disagree

20. We value clarity of communication, asking for confirmation to make sure we understand each other.

    a. strongly agree

    b. agree

    c. slightly agree

    d. slightly disagree

    e. disagree

    f. strongly disagree

21. When we have issues, we go directly to our teammates instead of going outside the team to vent or gain support.

    a. strongly agree

    b. agree

    c. slightly agree

    d. slightly disagree

    e. disagree

    f. strongly disagree

Number of responses for statements 19–21:

a.___ b.___ c.___ d.___ e.___ f.___

Your weighted score results:

Statements	Responses					
	a	b	c	d	e	f
1–3						
4–6						
7–9						
10–12						
13–15						
16–18						
19–21						
Total for each column (x)						
Weighted value (y)						
Weighted score (x) x (y)						
Grand Total						

Example of weighted score results:

Statements	Responses					
	a	b	c	d	e	f
1–3		1	1		1	
4–6	1			1		1
7–9		1	1			1
10–12			1	1	1	
13–15					1	2
16–18		2		1		
19–21			1	1		1
Total for each column (x)	1	4	4	4	3	5
Weighted value (y)	6	5	4	3	2	1
Weighted score (x) x (y)	1 x 6 =6	4 x 5 =20	4 x 4 =16	4 x 3 =12	3 x 2 = 6	5 x 1 = 5
Grand Total	65					

Interpretation of your total:

21–62: Your boat is rowing in different directions. Get help as fast as you can.

63–104: Your boat is taking the hard route. Get help before you get tired and lost.

105+: Your team is working in sync. Keep up the good work.

Appendix B

Rowers' Code Summary

1. Always Do What's Best for the Team.
Commit to your team.

2. Every Seat Has Equal Value.
Tap into the strengths of your peers.

3. Carry Your Load.
Be responsible.

4. Balance the Boat.
Attain the right mix.

5. Stay in Sync.
Realize that what you do and don't do affects others.

6. Lead by Example.
Trust in yourself and others.

7. Keep Everything in the Boat.
Work issues out directly with your teammates.

#1 Always Do What's Best for the Team.	Putting the interests of your team in front of your own. Rowing as "one boat" instead of everyone rowing in his or her own direction.	Commitment
#2 Every Seat Has Equal Value.	Treating others with respect. Acknowledging and trusting in each other's strengths.	Acknowledgment
#3 Carry Your Load.	Knowing and doing your share of what needs to be done.	Responsibility
#4 Balance the Boat.	Attaining the right mix of people and skills on your team to meet your goals.	Organizational and self-awareness
#5 Stay in Sync.	Timing is everything. Realizing that everything you do affects others. Knowing your bandwidth and the bandwidth of others.	Situational awareness
#6 Lead by Example.	Trusting in yourself and others. Sharing leadership responsibility.	Trust
#7 Keep Everything in the Boat.	Communicating clearly and honestly with your teammates.	Integrity

Are you up to the challenge?

Visit our Website at *www.rowerscode.com*:

♦ Print and display Rowers' Code posters.

♦ Print Rowers' Code bookmarks and distribute.

♦ Complete the team assessment (paper or online).

♦ Print pages featuring Rowers' Code helpful tools and tips.

♦ Invite a friend to learn the Rowers' Code and get in the winning boat with you.

♦ Register for a Rowers' Code offsite.

♦ Sign up for our free e-newsletter.

♦ Join our blogging community.

Is your team in sync?

If you are interested in teambuilding programs or speaking engagements based on the Rowers' Code, contact us at info@rowerscode.com or visit our Website at *www.rowerscode.com*.

Index

About the Authors

Marilyn Krichko created the Rowers' Code and founded the OARS Program teambuilding company in 1998 (now Criterion Consulting Solutions). Marilyn's innovative programs have helped many teams experience teambuilding during unique offsites, where they learn to row in an Olympic-style rowing boat and apply the Rowers' Code to their situations at work.

Prior to founding the OARS Program, Marilyn was an executive for a Swedish paper company, where she worked in an intense multilingual, multinational environment, requiring extensive teamwork and communication. She received her MBA in 1989 from the University of North Florida in Jacksonville, and has attended advanced studies in total quality management at the Chalmars University of Technology in Göteborg, Sweden. Marilyn is an avid rower at Lake Washington Rowing Club (LWRC).

Marilyn lives with her family in Seattle, where she is a corporate consultant and an avid rower.

Jane Rollinson is a well-known leader in the health-care industry, with more than 25 years of senior management experience. She has had responsibility for local, national, and international operations with the position of CFO, COO, president, vice president, and chief executive, as well as consulting with foreign governments on health-care issues. Jane's accomplishments include business start-ups, growth, and turnarounds. Her last executive position before joining Criterion Consulting Solutions was as a corporate turnaround specialist at UnitedHealthcare. Her contacts extend to executives at several Fortune 500 companies, who have been her customers for years. Jane sits on for-profit and several not-for-profit boards. Jane's extensive experience in finance, management, marketing, and organizational development helps her build teams and focus them on executing the requirements for unprecedented business success.

Jane and her husband, Brad, a PGA golf professional, and her son, Christian, reside in Ponte Vedra Beach, Florida.